THE RELIGIO-POLITICAL FACTIONS IN EARLY ISLAM

North-Holland Medieval Translations

volume 3

General Editor

RICHARD VAUGHAN

University of Hull

NORTH-HOLLAND PUBLISHING COMPANY – AMSTERDAM • OXFORD
AMERICAN ELSEVIER PUBLISHING COMPANY, INC. – NEW YORK

THE RELIGIO-POLITICAL FACTIONS IN EARLY ISLAM

By
JULIUS WELLHAUSEN

Edited by
R. C. OSTLE

Translated by
R.C. OSTLE and S.M. WALZER

1975

NORTH-HOLLAND PUBLISHING COMPANY – AMSTERDAM • OXFORD
AMERICAN ELSEVIER PUBLISHING COMPANY, INC. – NEW YORK

North-Holland ISBN for this Series: 0 7204 9000 6
North-Holland ISBN for this Volume: 0 7204 9005 7
American Elsevier ISBN: 0 444 10872 6

Publishers:

NORTH-HOLLAND PUBLISHING COMPANY – AMSTERDAM
NORTH-HOLLAND PUBLISHING COMPANY, LTD. – OXFORD

Sole distributors for the U.S.A. and Canada:

AMERICAN ELSEVIER PUBLISHING COMPANY, INC.
52 VANDERBILT AVENUE
NEW YORK, N.Y. 10017

This book was originally published in German, under the title:
„Die religiös-politischen Oppositionsparteien im alten Islam".

PRINTED IN THE NETHERLANDS

CONTENTS

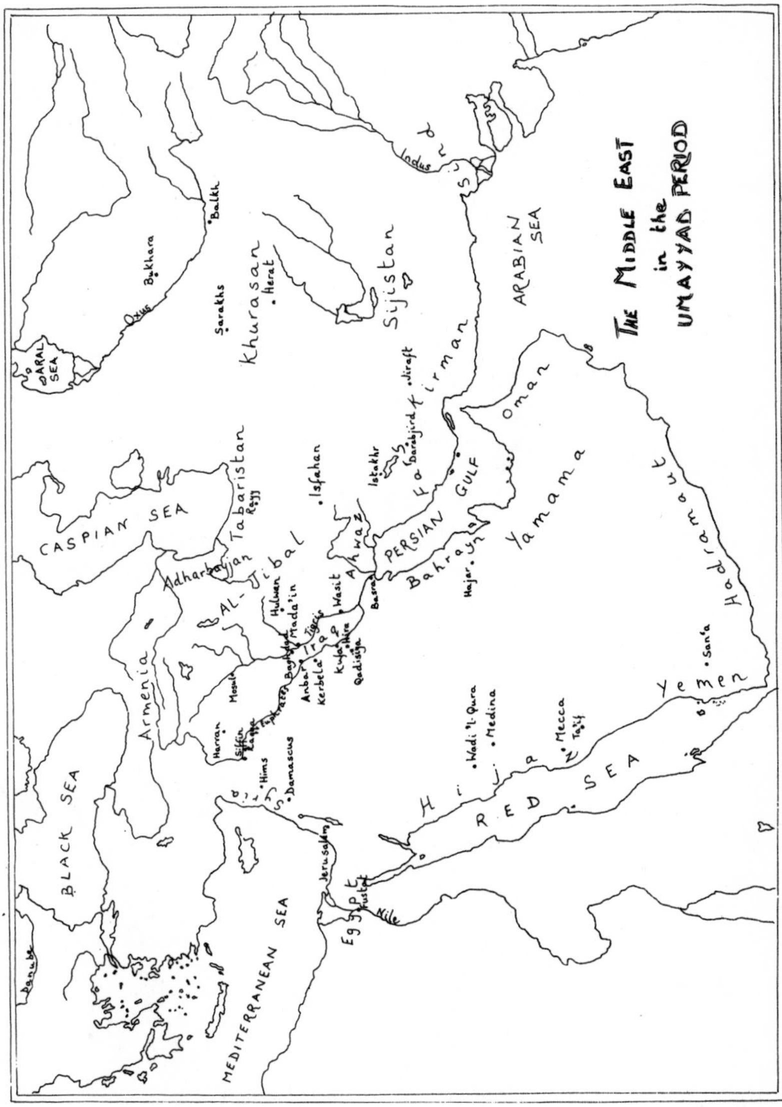
THE MIDDLE EAST
in the
UMAYYAD PERIOD
CASPIAN SEA
ARAL SEA
BLACK SEA
MEDITERRANEAN SEA
PERSIAN GULF
ARABIAN SEA
RED SEA
Danube
Nile
Euphrates
Tigris
Oxus
Indus
Sind
Armenia
Adharbayjan
Tabaristan
Rayy
AL-Jibal
Khurasan
Sarakhs
Herat
Balkh
Bukhara
Sijistan
Kirman
Jiraft
Fars
Istakhr
Darabjird
Isfahan
Ahwaz
Iraq
Baghdad
Mada'in
Hulwan
Wasit
Basra
Kufa
Hira
Qadisiya
Anbar
Kerbela
Mosul
Harran
Siffin
Raqqa
Syria
Hims
Damascus
Jerusalem
Egypt
Fustat
Bahrayn
Hajar
Yamama
Oman
Hijaz
Wadi 'l-Qura
Medina
Mecca
Ta'if
Yemen
San'a
Hadramaut

F O R E W O R D.

The translation of Julius Wellhausen's *Die religiös-politischen Oppositionsparteien im alten Islam* (Abhandlungen der Königlichen Gesellschaft der Wissenschaften zu Göttingen, V/5, 1901) was originally the suggestion of the late Dr. S.M. Stern, who intended to edit and revise the translation as he had done with the two volumes of Goldziher's *Muslim Studies*. The fact that he was sadly unable to do this is another small example of his numerous unfulfilled projects for which this field of study will be the poorer.

The original of this work appeared shortly before the much more comprehensive volume on the Omayyads, *Das arabische Reich und sein Sturz* familiar to every student of Islamic history and, not unnaturally, this shorter treatise on the early development of the Khawārij and the Shīʻa has tended to be overshadowed by the subsequent larger volume. However, the more limited scope of this book means that the material has not become outdated on quite such a wide scale, and it retains for this subject much of the value which it had as the most masterly study of its own time and for years to come.

Series II of the Leiden edition of Ṭabarī's *Annales* had been published for almost twenty years before Wellhausen produced this monograph on the early Islamic factions and he bases his findings primarily on one of the most exciting and attractive features of this part of Ṭabarī, the traditions of the Kūfan Azdite Abū Mikhnaf. While he is not entirely uncritical of Abū Mikhnaf as a historical source (see *The Arab Kingdom and its Fall*, reprint Beirut 1963, Preface IX-XII), because his was the oldest account of the sectarian rebellions in Kūfa and the least contaminated by intermediaries or geographical remoteness (see pp.5-7), his stories are the basis of Wellhausen's own re-creation of the highly confusing episodes of this remote period. The other later traditionists and chroniclers are used to complement or corroborate but not to contradict this primary source.

The method which emerges from the first three chapters is typical of the book as a whole: we begin with a dramatic paraphrase of the relevant events as narrated by Abū Mikhnaf in Ṭabarī, then the versions of later Islamic authorities are discussed and in most cases dismissed, taking full account of their religious and political prejudices. Finally, Wellhausen turns his critical attentions to the theories of his own contemporaries and predecessors such as Weil, Dozy, Brünnow and Müller. Although certain parts of the author's ideas and conclusions have been superseded by subsequent research (particularly in section II on the Shīʿa), this should not detract from a most rewarding feature of this book, that is Wellhausen's infectious enthusiasm for the chronicles with which he works. The drama and excitement of the tales of Abū Mikhnaf are communicated as directly as possible to the reader, the book is full of lengthy paraphrase and also direct quotations, on occasion quite lengthy. Along with the proliferation of the names of witnesses and the tribes involved in the rebellions and counter-rebellions, these factors combine to lend this work a flavour of the original chronicles such as is rarely found in a secondary source. For students who may have neither the time nor the linguistic experience necessary to read the original Ṭabarī, this should be a particular attraction. It cannot be claimed that this is a book which reads easily or fluently (in German or in English!), but usually the guiding hand of Wellhausen himself saves one from being submerged entirely in the bewildering succession of names and events through which he threads his way with clear-mindedness and coherence. In the company of such a master of the sources, one can afford to indulge the mild prejudice revealed in comments about Arab avarice and tribal temperament (pp.8-9)!

It is vital that readers, and students in particular, should read the text in close conjunction with the notes supplied at the end of each chapter, for it is there that the major findings of subsequent research are indicated. Many of these revisions were kindly supplied by Professor I.M. Lapidus of Berkeley, California, and these are indicated by (L). My own briefer additions are indicated by (Ed.), while Wellhausen's notes appear in their original form. The transliteration of names and places is based on the system used in the new edition of the Encyclopaedia of Islam, but with some simplifying modifications. Finally, thanks are due to Dr. R.R. Walzer and Dr. Jutta Jacobmeyer for help and suggestions which they gave in the translation of this book.

R.C.O.

November, 1974.

1 - THE KHAWĀRIJ

(Presented in the Session of 3rd August, 1901)

CHAPTER 1.

The Battle of Ṣiffīn had an aftermath of momentous significance in the camp of those who were victorious, but who were nevertheless denied the fruits of victory. A further step was taken along the course embarked on with the assassination of ʿUthmān.

Being in danger of defeat, the Syrians stuck Qur'āns on to the ends of their lances, following ʿAmr's advice. This produced the desired effect upon the Iraqis, in particular the pious Qur'ān readers. ʿAlī saw through the ruse, but was unable to prevent its taking effect, and was threatened when he tried to do so. He had to call a halt to the battle, and to bring back Ashtar who was advancing to victory. So as not to expose ʿAlī himself to danger, the latter reluctantly obeyed the repeated command but only after giving vent to his anger against those "pious rascals"[1] who forced him to give up a certain victory. After ʿAlī had been compelled to submit to this, Ashʿath b. Qays, the chief of the Kinda of Kūfa, offered to go to Muʿāwiya to plan the next steps. Muʿāwiya proposed that each side should choose a representative, and that those chosen should decide to whom the hegemony was due, basing their decision on the Qur'ān.[2] Ashʿath accepted this proposal and put it to the Iraqis. They at once declared their agreement without consulting ʿAlī. The Syrians immediately chose ʿAmr b. al-ʿĀṣ, as their representative and the Iraqis chose Abū Mūsā. ʿAlī protested against the latter in vain, but the same neutrality which made him unacceptable to ʿAlī was what recommended him to the others: (who said)

"We have now fallen into the very situation against which he (Abū Mūsā) warned us."[3]

Thereupon a treaty was made in the Iraqi's camp according to which ʿAlī had to undergo humiliation not unlike that suffered by the Prophet at Ḥudaybiya in similar circumstances.[4] The two sides pledged themselves to lay down their arms and to accept the judgement; the noblest men of the two armies added their signatures. Only Ashtar was obdurate in his refusal, and slandered Ash'ath.

In fact, Ash'ath himself was burning with rage, but he continued to play the role of the busily efficient broker. On the completion of the treaty, he rode amongst the Iraqi army and informed them all of its contents. He came to a group of Tamīmites from Baṣra, amongst whom was 'Urwa b. Udayya al-Ḥanẓalī, and read the agreement to them. When 'Urwa realised that the decision as to who should rule the Theocracy was to lie in the hands of two men, he cried out in anger: "The decision rests with God alone!", and struck the back of Ash'ath's mount with his sword, causing it to leap away wildly. Ash'ath's tribal supporters from Yemen flew into a rage on his behalf against the Tamīmites, but their leaders intervened and calmed Ash'ath. But when the Iraqis made their way home, dissatisfaction became widespread with the outcome of the battle. The selfsame people who had urged 'Alī to halt the conflict, now blamed him because the future of the Theocracy depended on the opinions of two negotiators. An intense quarrel arose between them and his loyal followers. The former reproached the latter saying that they took 'Alī's side even though he was in the wrong, and that they were servants of men,[5] just like the Syrians who went with Mu'āwiya through thick and thin, without questioning whether he was right or not. The entry into Kūfa became lamentable, almost more miserable than that of a defeated army, because the victory gained by such costly bloodshed had been given away so foolishly. The laments for the dead raised by their families cut 'Alī to the quick, and he was wounded by the open derision of those who were inclined to support 'Uthmān. The traitors rejoiced, while the loyal followers were in distress. Twelve thousand men deserted 'Alī and did not accompany him into Kūfa, but went instead to the small town called Ḥarūrā',[6] with the taḥkīm as their watchword: "The ḥukm (that is "the power of decision") rests with God alone!" Thereafter, they were named the Muḥakkimūn. Usually they are called the Ḥarūrites, or more generally, the Khawārij.[7,8]

1. See note on p.16.(Ed.)

2. More recently discovered Khārijite sources make clear that the issue put to arbitration was whether or not the previous Caliph ʿUthmān had been unjustly murdered, and therefore whether Muʿāwiya's claim, as a close relative of ʿUthmān's, for vengeance was justified. The immediate issue was not ʿAlī's title to the Caliphate, though the arbitration would in effect be a trial of his legitimacy. See L. Veccia Vaglieri, "Il conflitto ʿAlī - Muʿāwiya e la secessione khārigita riesaminati alla luce di fonti ibāḍite." Annali Istituto Universitario Orientale di Napoli, IV (1952), pp.1-94. (L)

3. See Ṭab.I, p.3333, 11.11-12. These were the words of al- Ashʿath, Zayd b. Ḥuṣayn al- Ṭāʾī, and Misʿar b. Fadakī, who forced ʿAlī to accept Abū Mūsā as a negotiator. (Ed.)

4. In 628 Muḥammad attempted to make the first Muslim pilgrimage to Mecca. The Meccans refused him entry to the city, and at Ḥudaybiya negotiated a treaty which failed to include mention of Muḥammad's claim to be the prophet of God and imposed unequal obligations upon the Muslim side. On the other hand, Muḥammad gained recognition as a diplomatic and political equal of Mecca and the right to make the pilgrimage in the following year. (L)

5. i.e. Servants of men and not of God. (Ed.)

6. Arūrītai, Theoph. p.421, 1.18, p.424, 1.9, p.439, 1.13. Ed. de Boor.

7. The verb from which this name is derived usually means "to take the field against someone", and commonly "to rise in revolt"; it is also used in an absolute sense (Ṭab.II, p.33, 1.6). But in the cases in point, it means much more "to secede from the community" (jamāʿa) (p.543, 1.20, p.889, 1.5). A mixture of Charigitai and Arūrītai appears as Charūrgitai in Theoph. p.347, 1.30. Perhaps the term Khawārij is best rendered in English as Nonconformists or Separatists.

8. The Ḥarūrites, later called Khārijites, were at first secessionists and not rebels. They had held that Mu'āwiya was a rebel, that according to the Qur'ān, XLIX, 9, rebels are outlaws until they return to obedience to God, and that arbitration was thus a religious error because no one had the right to substitute a human decision for God's clear pronouncement. The Ḥarūrites, however, did not wish to attack 'Alī for his acquiescence in the arbitration agreement, but they wished to secede from the community to protect their principles. See L. Veccia Vaglieri, "Sulla denominazione Ḫawāriǧ", Rivista degli Studi Orientali, XXVI (1951), pp.41-46; Vaglieri, Il conflitto 'Alī-Mu'āwiya, pp.31-38; Encyclopaedia of Islam, new edition, q.v. 'Alī b. Abī Ṭālib; Ḥarūrā'. (L)

CHAPTER 2.

So runs the account of Abū Mikhnaf, which is by far the oldest we possess. Following on from Weil, all later scholars are unanimous in finding it a quite incomprehensible story. They suspect that there were traitors on the Iraqi side with whom Mu'āwiya and 'Amr planned the ruse beforehand. One can imagine the names of the traitors: Abū Mūsā and Ash'ath.

Abū Mūsā al-Ash'arī was one of the oldest of the Companions of the Prophet, a man with a deep and thorough knowledge of the Qur'ān and altogether a very distinguished person. For twelve or thirteen years, from 17-29 h./638-49, he was governor of Baṣra during a very disturbed and highly eventful period. In the year 29 h./649 'Uthmān took away his governorship to replace him with a younger relative. After this he seems to have taken up residence in Kūfa and to have gained popularity there. The Kūfans wanted him as governor in place of the Umayyad Sa'īd b.'Āṣ, whom they prevented from entering the city, and they persuaded 'Uthmān to agree. Naturally Abū Mūsā was no friend of 'Uthmān who had removed him without reason from his position in Baṣra and had only placed him in Kūfa under coercion. Had it not been so, the Kūfans would not have chosen him, for they were very antagonistic towards the Caliph. Abū Mūsā did not, however, approve of the murder of 'Uthmān; rather he foresaw its evil consequences and tried to make the Kūfans stay neutral and not to stand in 'Alī's way. But events took a different turn and he was pushed to one side. However, he was able to remain undisturbed in Kūfa, nor indeed was he alone in his political views.[1]

He was quite open about his political position, and 'Alī knew exactly where he stood with him: this was the reason why 'Alī objected to him as an arbiter. Why then was he suspected of dishonesty at Ṣiffīn, of collusion with the Syrians? It seems that the suspicion was based merely on the fact that he was there when he was needed.[2] Moreover, there is nothing strange in Arab practice for a distinguished man to refuse to stay at home when his men are going to battle, nor, equally, for him to stay aloof from the conflict if he is dubious about the aims for which it is being fought. Abū Mūsā was not hand in glove with Muʿāwiya and made no show of friendship to him at the court of arbitration. He later fled from the Syrians to Mecca and went in fear of his life when they were advancing towards the city under the command of Busr. In this civil war he stood between the two sides, like so many others. He was neither for ʿAlī nor for Muʿāwiya, but was for ʿAbdalla b. ʿUmar. Thus it is quite understandable that the Kūfans should decide to choose him, their former governor, as their trusted representative, at the time when they themselves were beginning to waver: "We have now fallen into the very situation against which he warned us".

Therefore there only remains the charge of treachery against Ashʿath. According to the evidence of the events at Nujayr,[3] he was much more suited to the role of traitor than Abū Mūsā. Furthermore, most of the blame was attached to him by Weil, Dozy, Brünnow and Müller.[4] Showing prudent anticipation of a possible unfavourable outcome, the Syrians are supposed to have said to him beforehand: "If we are in danger of being beaten, then we shall stick Qur'āns on to the ends of our lances. Then you must see to it that the battle is broken off!" According to this account, it is supposed to have been thanks to him that the Iraqis understood the signal and complied with it. Müller, quite in the spirit of Sayf b. ʿUmar, supplies "the Rabble" as his accomplices - obviously being correctly convinced that the Iraqis would not merely have followed his advice and danced to his tune without any further thought.

Ashʿath did not yet interfere at this stage of the proceedings; he did so only when ʿAlī had given the command to stop fighting. It was not Ashʿath but other people who were slandered by Ashtar when he was obliged to sheath his sword. Thus at least goes the account of Abū Mikhnaf. It is true that Dīnawarī and Yaʿqūbī, later, much less reliable historians, told a different story, but they are simply converting their suppositions into facts and cannot be allowed to contradict the account of Abū Mikhnaf, who had no reason to save Ash'ath's face. Ya'qūbī says that Ash'ath was won over to Mu'āwiya's side and forced 'Alī to call Ashtar back. The Yemenīs were on Ash'ath's side and, on this occasion, there was nearly a clash between him and Ashtar. But those same Yemenīs from Kūfa were also 'Alī's main supporters (see The Kāmil p.539), and it was at the head of their most powerful tribes, the Hamdān and the Madhhij, that Ashtar was victorious at Ṣiffīn. One finds here in Ya'qūbī a version which is reminiscent of the episode also related by Abū Mikhnaf where Ash'ath quarrelled with the Tamīmite 'Urwa b.Udayya. The Yemenīs sided with Ash'ath against the Tamīmites, and there was nearly a clash between them and the Tamīmites. Müller's remark (I, p.325) is revealing, when he suggests that the basic reason for the trouble at Ṣiffīn was the well-known, universally accepted tribal jealousy between North and South Arabs. If Ya'qūbī is correct, then Ash'ath roused the anger of his South Arabian troops in the armies against the large numbers of North Arabians amongst 'Alī's associates, in particular, Mālik. Unwittingly, Müller contradicts Ya'qūbī in this. If he were correct, then Ashtar would have had to be a northern Arab, but he was a well-known Yemenī.

Ash'ath proved busy and enthusiastic in the subsequent events on the completion of the treaty. After the decision to halt the battle, he offered to be an arbiter, and was appointed. He went to Mu'āwiya, and accepted the proposal to set up a court of arbitration. On the basis of this proposal, he did what he could to arrange a written treaty between the two sides; as a result, he was then slandered by Ashtar (but not previously). Then he proclaimed the contents of the treaty throughout the Iraqi camp. This was the occasion of the first protest on the part of Udayya.[5] But where did the treachery lie in these actions of Ash'ath? He did not lead the current, but simply allowed himself to be carried along by it. He pushed himself forward and made himself important, so increasing the unpleasantness of the situation, but that does not constitute treachery. Nothing prevented him from defecting to Mu'āwiya, as did many other Kūfans, and from taking his traitor's reward. Instead he stayed by ʻAlī and, as before, took up a very distinguished position in Kūfa. His sons and grandsons followed his example and had no sympathy at all for the Syrian hegemony. Of course Yaʻqūbī repeated all manner of subsequent devilry about him, but, according to Abū Mikhnaf, he did no more at a later stage than he had done at Ṣiffīn: he pushed himself forward in order to occupy a prominent position as a Sayyid. According to The Kāmil, on more than one occasion he proved to be a friend of ʻAlī: he told him about the evil-doings of the Khawārij and warned him about Ibn Muljam.[6] Finally, one might ask, what reward did he ask for, or expect, from his supposed treachery? He got no money; and no Arab performs such a duty without money. Dozy attributes the following motive to him which he is quite happy to take as generally and currently accepted, inappropriate though it is:[7] since Ashʻath was a former heathen, in his heart he wished to take revenge on Islam which had treated him badly at Nujayr.[8] But in fact it was through Islam that he had obtained his position in Kūfa, a position which he had never held at Nujayr. Generally Islam was considered from its political side, according to which it had united the Arabs and led them to rule the world. One could willingly forget the past for the sake of the glorious present. Ashʻath had at least as much reason to do so as any other of the Ahl al-Ridda, who made up the majority of the inhabitants of Kūfa and Baṣra. Besides, revenge for Nujayr is not a sufficient motive for this particular action, i.e. treason against ʻAlī in favour of Muʻāwiya.

The search for traitors is vain and also quite superfluous. It is not at all unlikely that the brandishing of Qur'āns at the height of danger was an improvisation on the part of the wily ʻAmr b.al-ʻĀṣ. The idea was obvious, and probably had some precedent.[9] Lances always served as flagstaffs, and the Qur'ān was the banner of Islam. In this way the Syrians wanted to show the Iraqis that they were fighting against people whose banner was no less than theirs - the Word of God.[10] The Iraqis needed nothing more to understand this, and no wonder it made an impression on them. The struggle for the ruling position in the Theocracy had dragged them into the conflict against ʻUthmān, then against ʻĀ'isha and the Baṣrans, and now against Muʻāwiya and the Syrians. The jamā'a, the unified body of the Theocracy, was split up into the shī'a (party) of 'Alī, and the shī'a of Mu'āwiya. This result was a highly dubious one, for Islam had wished to put an end to the fatal divisions and internal strife of the Arabs, and had actually done so. It enjoined the Community to revere its peace and unity as something very precious. In the course of the negotiations between the two armies, which lay encamped opposite each other at Ṣiffīn for a long time, it became clear in addition that the Syrians were just as God-fearing as the Iraqis, and were equally convinced of their own rights. It is understandable that the Iraqis became somewhat uncertain in their point of view, and that they gave in to the suggestion of sticking the Qur'āns on to the lances on the spur of the moment. They were more irritable and more given to changes of mood than Northern Europeans are, for example. They were in the grip of a religious dilemma, and did not act from political or military considerations.

---

1. Abū Mūsā led the Kūfans to accept 'Alī as the new Caliph, but he maintained a neutral position in the disputes which broke out between 'Alī and the Meccan faction led by Ṭalḥa and al-Zubayr, which culminated in the Battle of the Camel. He was then removed from the governorship but continued to be recognised as a leading neutralist. (L)

2. He was in Urd, between Tadmur and Ruṣāfa, that is quite near the scene of the battle. (Ṭab.I, p. 3,334). For a charming account see Dīnawarī, pp.205s. Ed. Guirgass.

3. After Muḥammad's death, Ash'ath rebelled against Medinian authority. He was beseiged at Nujayr and surrendered in return for amnesty. (L)

4. For these authors and their works, see the bibliography. (Ed.)

5. Udayya only protested against the court of arbitration, and not against the halting of the battle. He also came to his senses too late, but earlier than the others.

6. ʿAlī's assassin. (L)

7. e.g. also in the case of Muslim b.ʿUqba. (See E.I. old edition, Vol.III, p.757.) (Ed.)

8. See note 3.

9. Ṭab.I, p.3,186, 3,188s. p.876, l.19. Compare the verse in Dīnawarī p.182, l.9. A later example is in Nicephorus p.37, l.4, ed. de Boor.

10. Raising the Qur'ān on lances was not a common gesture, but since the basic disagreement turned on the application of Qur'ānic verses in the dispute over the legitimacy of ʿUthmān's murder, raising the Qur'ān on lances was easily understood as an appeal to discussions. Vaglieri, Il conflitto ʿAlī-Muʿāwiya, pp.24-26. (L)

CHAPTER 3.

Those who called the tune for the Iraqis were the Qur'ān readers; they, before all others, bowed to the Qur'ān as the true mediator and arbiter in case of strife amongst the Muslims; they carried the people along with them and forced 'Alī himself to submit. They are supposed to have subsequently raised the loudest protest against the treaty and the court of arbitration, and the Khawārij are supposed to have sprung from them. Thus relates Abū Mikhnaf in somewhat dry terms, according to Ṭabarī, I, p.3330, and this is the most reliable account.

Brünnow[1] considers it impossible that there was such a sudden change within the same circle of people. He attributes the contradictory modes of action to different circles: according to him, the Qur'ān readers had stopped the conflict and then the Khawārij protested against it; the latter are said to have been Bedouins. But what took place between Ash'ath and 'Urwa b. Udayya as related by Abū Mikhnaf would show clearly that dissatisfaction with the treaty did not spring from the Qur'ān readers. This event is quite immaterial, and merely a prelude to the sudden general changes which followed later. The interest which it entails is of a formal nature, namely, who first raised the shout of the taḥkīm. Later this became an oft-discussed point of dispute which was answered in many different ways.[2] But, besides this, how can Brünnow justify considering 'Urwa b. Udayya and the old Khawārij in general as "Bedouins" and how can he bring these "genuine Bedouin Arabs" into a position of exclusive opposition to the Qur'ān readers, when he himself had described the former as being so zealous in their piety, and steeped in the study of the Qur'ān? He starts from false hypotheses. In one sense, the Arabs of Kūfa and Baṣra were nearly all Bedouins, that is to say they hailed from desert tribes. In this respect, there is nothing special to be said about the Khawārij. But they had in fact lost their contact with the desert tribes through the

Hijra, through emigration to the garrison cities, and inscribing their names on the lists of the army.[3] The *Hijra* represented a casting off of the Bedouin way of life; as *Muhājira* they stood opposed to the *A'rāb*.[4] They had become military stipendaries of the state, or *Muqātila*; they were raised and encouraged by the success of their *Jihād*, by the great deeds of God wrought through their hands. Since they now lived a life of leisure in urban centres, they turned their interests towards the public affairs of the Theocracy. The true Bedouins, who carried on their old way of life, remained far removed from religio-political activity and factionalism,[5] just like the inhabitants of the villages. Islam set no great store by them and treated them as camel thieves. *'Arabī* became a pejorative term for an uncivilised, irreligious man. If such a person came to Kūfa or Baṣra, he ran the risk of being ridiculed.[6] Those *Muqātila* with names inscribed in the *Dīwān* who were resident in the garrison towns, would certainly dislike the title. It was considered disgraceful if they were sent back to their tribes in the former Arab lands; it was a punishment, a banishment.[7] There is nothing to lead one to believe that the oldest *Khawārij* who were recruited from Kūfa and Baṣra were any different in this respect from the other Kūfans and Baṣrans. On the contrary, whilst the others retained for quite a long time the blood-relationship and the old system of genealogy based on kinship, they were much less concerned about this, or at any rate it was not fundamental to them. They cut themselves off from their families, but if they were caught by them again, as was often the case, then they stopped being *Khārijites*. They did not adopt the Arabian deserts as places of refuge, but non-Arab regions: the area of Jūkhā on the other side of the Tigris, Ahwāz, Media and Fārs.[8] Brünnow would have been correct if he had not gone beyond the assertion that the *Khawārij* did not come from the Quraysh or the Thaqīf or the Anṣār, but that they first arose amongst the politically under-priveleged. As a rule, it was only after the *Ridda* that such people were properly incorporated into tribes from Kūfa and Baṣra, as a result of the Islamic Conquests.[9]

Equally, Brünnow seems to have his own ideas about the Qur'ān readers themselves. (*Qurrā'*, sing. *Qāri'*).[10] They cannot be considered as having maintained a consistent position: they were men whose role is very difficult to define; even figures such Qays b. Sa'd, Hishām b. 'Utba and Ibn Budayl were occasionally included amongst their number. They did not belong to any political faction with a definite programme, and they were to be found amongst Syrians and Iraqis alike; the Iraqi Qur'ān readers mostly supported 'Alī and rode out to battle at his side, but four hundred of them held back and stayed at home. This happened because of the famous 'Abdalla b. Mas'ūd who seemed to hold the same views as Abū Mūsā. (Dīnaw, p.175). They were in league with the religious lawyers, the Fuqahā',[11] and in relation to them occupied a position rather like the outer circumference of two concentric circles. But for preference they were not given to theoretical and literary inclinations. (Ṭab.II, p.564, ll.16s.) The Qur'ān, from which they had their name, was not really to be studied, but was more for practice and edification. Its themes were recited as prayers, in the mosque as well as in small chambers. The readers, or the reciters, could also be described as those who prayed. The Qur'ān was forever on their lips, they knew large sections of it by heart and declaimed it with vigour, both publicly and privately, loudly and softly, by day and by night. They were called "those with dusty brows"[12] because of the zeal with which they struck their brows on the ground during prayers. (Sur.XLVIII, v.29). But they did not keep the peace, nor did they remain in a state of quiet piety. True to the nature of the Theocracy, they eagerly directed and advised in public affairs. They sought and gained influence over the masses. When the revolt against 'Uthmān was prepared in Kūfa, they were the most vociferous group. Apart from being the aristocracy of the oldest Companions of the Prophet, they also stood out as the chief offenders in the fateful murder of the Caliph. As good Muslims they also took part in battles. They made speeches before the fighting in order to rouse people. Although they were not in the front line of the action, they knew that the most effective theology lay in helping God with swords. (Ṭab.II, p.1086). Already at Yamāma the ones who had memorized and could recite the Qur'ān were considered most distinguished. Those pious Medīnans can be thought of as the forerunners of the later Qur'ān readers. In the Battle of the Camel, then again at Ṣiffīn, and in all subsequent conflicts, especially against al-Ḥajjāj, the Qur'ān readers were prominent.

They were not the essential instigators or motivators of the broad lines of actions, but they engendered the enthusiasm that moved the masses. They seldom swam against the stream, but were more like choir leaders, the barometer, and the mouthpiece of public opinion. Opposition provided the most fertile ground for their criticisms and complaints. They flourished for that reason less in Syria than in Iraq; in Kūfa and Baṣra, they were of the greatest significance. The banners which they followed were God, the Qur'ān, the Sunna, the law, and the tradition. They were not reliable as a political faction. Nor were they trustworthy supporters for a leader whom they themselves had placed in a position of power.

If such was the nature of the Qur'ān readers, then one must allow that they could well be the breeding-ground for the Khawārij. They display extreme piety, and portray it in the same manner: the Qur'ān is forever on their lips, they pray over it and contemplate it day and night. Their eyes are red from lack of sleep and their brows wounded from endless prostrations. They reflect on the principles of their religion, and dispute them in skilful argument. A particular mark of enthusiastic ascetics in those days was the burnous, the long cape. A group of such people wearing these long hoods or capes, under the command of ʿAbdalla b. Shajara al-Sulamī, were amongst the very earliest Khawārij.

Must one now establish separate identities and aims of the Readers and the Khawārij, merely to attribute trends towards a decline or rise in fortune to different factions? Is it then inconceivable that the same people first allowed their consciences to be confused, and then found them again? On the contrary, without that the Khawārij cannot be understood at all. First, after a fall from grace they regained that energy and certitude which they later held to be the essence of piety. They considered their past vacillation as a disgraceful sin, and now turned all their energy towards expiating it. It was repentance which caused them to appear, and to act.[13] They themselves made good this repentance through action, and they asked the same of ʿAlī and of others. On every occasion, this was clear. If it were not so, if the hall-mark of the Khawārij were to pursue consistently the consequences of their original actions, then Mālik al-Ashtar, their hostile enemy, would have the best claim to the title. He alone had not fallen into error: he had first raised the protest against the treaty with the Syrians, and had remained adamant. Finally, early tradition states not only in general terms that the Khawārij came from the circle of the Qur'ān readers, but specific names are given. Miṣ'ar b. Fadakī al-Tamīmī and Zayd. b. Ḥuṣayn al-Ṭā'ī, with other Qur'ān readers, forced 'Alī to make a treaty with the Syrians, and threatened him with 'Uthmān's fate if he did not obey the order to recognize God's book as the arbiter. The same two men later appear as the most extreme Khārijites. Such a definite declaration cannot be contradicted by mere suppositions, which in themselves are without foundation.

---

1. In his Doctorate thesis on the Khārijites, Strasbourg, 1884.

2. Dīnaw. p.210. The Kāmil, p.538, ll.16ss., p.539, ll.1ss., p.544, ll.1ss. Compare also The Kāmil p.565, l.11, where the story is told of the wounding by a Khārijite of a peace negotiator's horse on another occasion altogether.

3. Yaḥyā b. Ādam, Kitāb al-Kharāj p.59.

4. Ṭab.II, p.864, l.9.

5. The Ahl al-Ahwā' (The Kāmil p.546, l.7).

6. Ṭab.II, p.94s., p.565, l.5, p.568, l.11, p.590, l.6, p.825, l.11 Agh. vol.XVII, p.111, l.24.

7. This is shown by the story of the Ṭā'ī 'Abdalla b. Khalīfa, Ṭab.I, pp.3280s., II, pp.148ss.

8. The Khawārij did settle in Arabia itself, particularly in Yamāma and in Yemen, amongst sedentary non-nomadic people. However, that happened only at a later date, and does not concern us here.

9. Naturally we have a certain amount of information about the origins of the leaders only. There were many Tamīmites amongst them: thus from Baṣra, where the Tamīmites in general predominated, came Miṣʻar b. Fadakī, Ḥurqūṣ b. Zuhayr, ʻUrwa b. Udayya and his brother Abū Bilāl; from Kūfa came Shabath b. Ribʻī (who soon withdrew), Mustawrid and Hilāl b. ʻUllāfa, these last two being from the Taym Ribāb who were affiliated to the Tamīm. But there were also many from other tribes. Amongst other Muḍarites were Farwa b. Nawfal al-Ashjaʻī, Shurayḥ b. (Abī)'Awfā al-ʻAbsī, ʻAbdalla b. Shajara al-Sulamī (Ṭab.I, p.3377, p.3382, Dīnawarī p.216, l.13, p.221, l.6), Hamza b. Sinān al-Asadī, (Ṭab. p.3364, Dīn. p.215, l.17) and several Muḥāribites (p.3309s., p.3361s). From the Ṭayyi came Zayd b. Ḥusayn, Muʻā<u>dh</u> b. Juwayn, Ṭarafa b. ʻAdī b. Ḥātim. Amongst other Yemenīs were Yazīd b. Qays al-Arhabī (who soon withdrew), Ibn Wahb al-Rāsibī, the first Caliph, and Ibn Muljam al-Murādī, the murderer of ʻAlī. At first only a few of the Rabīʻa came forward, for example Ibn Kawā al-Yashkūrī (who later withdrew); later things became much different. Originally <u>Kh</u>ārijites are not generally found among the Baṣran Azdites, because the Azd immigrated to Baṣra only subsequently. The most distinguished men of the great tribes of Tamīm, Bakr, and Hamdān in Kūfa were nominated as the first three leaders of the Ḥarūrites.

10. Or at least seems to have had when he wrote his dissertation, of which, moreover, he need not be ashamed.

11. <u>Fuqahā'</u> is used anachronistically here. Early Muslim scholars did not make the distinctions which followed later as religious studies became more specialized. (L)

12. This explains the word "Dreckstirnen" on p.1, translated there as "pious rascals". (Ed.)

13. One sees the Muslim sense of "repentance" in Ṭab.II, p.332, l.2s.

C H A P T E R 4.

Very briefly, one may consider at this point a recently revived hypothesis which tries to trace the source of the Khawārij to the Sabā'iyya, along the lines of Sayf b. 'Umar's theory.[1] The leaders of the first Khawārij, or at least some of them, participated in the opposition against both 'Uthmān's governor and 'Uthmān himself, and they all claimed responsibility for his murder, considering this a point of honour amongst themselves: therefore, according to Sayf, they must have been Sabā'ites. He names specifically some of them who were prominent at Ḥarūrā' and at Nahrawān, including Ibn Muljam - but Ashtar completely upsets the theory. In fact, the title Sabā'ī was consistently applied only to the Shī'ites, not just as an extreme sect but as a pejorative name for them all.[2] The Khawārij themselves used the name to slander their Shī'ite opponents in Kūfa. (Ṭab.II, p.43, l.13). If one wanted to assume that the Sabā'iyya were the real assassins of 'Uthmān, and therefore the common root both of the Shī'a and of the Khawārij, then it remains to be established why the name previously was applied only to the extreme Shī'a. That would prove that the Khawārij only became Khawārij by defecting from the Sabā'iyya whom they, the Khawārij, are supposed originally to have been. Thus one is led back to the conclusion that their origin as Khawārij was at Ṣiffīn, and the events at Ṣiffīn must have made this clear. Furthermore, I have already demonstrated that the movement against 'Uthmān did not emerge from the Sabā'iyya, and that, in that affair, they were not as significant as Sayf would have them. However, I did not wish to use this argument in order to cut short the discussion about their relations with the Khawārij from the very beginning.[3]

The Khawārij are not weeds furtively sown by the Jew Ibn Sabā', but true sons of Islam. They were in earnest about their conception of the Theocracy and introduced nothing strange or peculiar to it. They did not start off as a small clandestine sect, but in the full public eye and on the broadest of foundations - namely, that of the general feeling which swept through the Iraqi army at Ṣiffīn. They were most numerous at the outset, and it was then that they were the least clearly defined. They came and went in a constant state of flux. It was impossible to know exactly who belonged to them, and some were surprised that Ashtar was not of their number. Their origins were essentially very different from those of the ʿAbbāsid and Fāṭimid parties. They did not have to resort to conspiracy and widespread propaganda, and were not held together by a secret complex organization. They had only principles, but these were always well-known to the people, and attracted supporters without their seeking them. However, the ones who actually took part in the subsequent action were always very few in number. They constantly took in new recruits. When the flame was stamped out in one area, it would burst out again elsewhere without any visible communication.[4] Tension reigned everywhere and was ready to explode. This is an indication of how deeply ingrained it was in the nature of Islam and the Theocracy.

---

1. He is Ṭabarī's chief source of information on ʿAbdalla b. Sabā' ; see Ṭab.I, pp.2941 ff. (Ed.)

2. Ṭab.II, p.43, p.136, l.16, p.623, l.14, p.651, l.7, p.703, l.17, p.704, l.11. Ṭab.III, p.29.

3. The Sabā'iyya were an extreme Shīʿite sect founded by ʿAbdalla b. Sabā' which must date from the latter part of the first Muslim century. Second century traditionalists, projecting disputes of their own day back to the time of the early Caliphate, assign a pernicious role in community affairs to this sect. B. Lewis, The Origins of Ismailism, p.25; E.I. (new edition), vol.I, p.51. (L)

4. Hence the doctrine of the fatarāt, the eclipse of the belief. (Agh. vol.XX, p.98) (See E.I. new edition, vol.II, p.865. Ed.)

CHAPTER 5.

The general source of the schism within Islam was the revolt against ʿUthmān: for God against the Caliph, for Law and Justice against folly and misrule. This formula could be applied not only to ʿUthmān but also to every other ruler who deviated from the right path. The Khawārij used it against ʿAlī to withdraw from his Shīʿa, so becoming Khawārij. The revolution which had brought ʿAlī to power could not be brought to a halt for his sake when he took a false step. One may find it impudent that the Khawārij reproached him for this step, when it was they who had made him take it, and then at once demanded that he **repudiate** his actions, although, as a ruler, it was almost impossible for him to do so. But logically it was not inconsistent. Willingly or not, ʿAlī had made a pact with the devil (i.e. Muʿāwiya) and then was unwilling to break that pact. He surrendered the Divine Right, which had caused the struggle against ʿUthmān and Muʿāwiya, so that he could keep a treaty with men which did not recognise that Right. Thus he had cut the ground from under his feet and lost the Caliphate. All those who supported him in spite of that would be idolizing his person. They were not concerned with the affairs of God but with the affairs of ʿAlī, just as the Syrians were concerned with the affairs of Muʿāwiya. Their position was none other than that of the Syrians, and no more tenable. If they waited for the verdict of the court of arbitration, then they would renounce that characteristic, determined, religio-political conviction which was essential for every Muslim in the Theocracy. Thus it was that they began to be ashamed of ʿUthmān's murder, for they lacked divine sanction but, equally, they could not make up their minds simply to exclude the Syrians from the community of Islam. The Khawārij came to know ʿAlī and his supporters better and better. The Law was only a pretext for him; he wanted power. This had certainly been the case from the outset, and had not just become so at a later stage.

Therefore, as their name implies, the Khawārij are an avowed revolutionary faction and, of course, a pious revolutionary faction. They do not emerge from Arabism, but from Islam, and their relation to those virtuosi of Islamic piety, the Qur'ān readers, formally resembles that of the Jewish Zealots to the Pharisees.[1] However, there remains the material difference that the Zealots fought for the fatherland, but the Khawārij only for God.

In the Theocracy, piety generally has a political slant, and this is so to the greatest extent amongst the Khawārij. God forbids His people to keep silent if His commandments on earth are abused. Not only must they personally do good and avoid doing evil, but they must see to it that this happens in all cases. They must order good deeds and forbid evildoing. Public action against injustice is the duty of the individual. He must express his convictions by word and deed. While this principle is common to all Muslims, to act recklessly upon it at all times is characteristic of the Khawārij.

The individual's duty to help God if He is insulted leads to conflict with authority. The Theocracy suffers from an inherent contradiction which, while not exclusive to it, yet affects it in a particular way. Rule over men belongs only to God: a human claim to it, a mulk (kingship), is sacrilegious. In this respect, no man has rights over another which are exclusive and more or less hereditary. An authority is only lawful if, and so long as, it rules in God's name and according to His will. Thus it is subordinate to the Dīn (the religion) and has to stand up to the criticism of the Dīn. This is the negative pole of the Theocracy but it also has a positive one. It founded the Jamā'a, an externally organized community of all Muslims, where peace and unity without anarchy reign, and, for this purpose, an Imām is placed at its head as a symbol of the unity of all the Muslim people. First, this was the Prophet as the almighty representative of God, then it was the Caliph as his successor who possessed similar hallowed authority (if only in a derived way) and his authority was passed on to his designated officials. In this contradiction between Dīn and Jamā'a, between the duty to put God and the Law above all and the duty to remain in the community, to obey the Imām, the

Khawārij decided to take the side of Dīn. As to what constitutes Dīn, essentially, they agree with the rest and are of like mind on the important points.[2] They differ only in the energy through which they allow religion to dominate every other consideration and make no compromise. There is no Jamā'a at the expense of religion, for the former is held together only by habit and external order and contains a proportionate number of wheat and tares. The Khawārij do not acknowledge the Jamā'a, which is only legalized in an historical sense by the fact of its existence. Only sincere Muslims belong to the true community, regardless of whether they are aristocratic or humble, Arab or Mawlā, and the foremost position belongs to the most pious. For that reason, they do not hesitate to tear the community apart. They take pride in the murder of 'Uthmān and they erect into a Shibboleth the confession of this fundamental act of revolution. They put every doubtful customer to the test with a most painful trial (Imtiḥān). They unashamedly shed the blood of their Muslim enemies. Their Jihād, the holy war which they wage, is no longer directed against the heathen but against the Catholic Muslims. For they consider these as the worst heathens,[3] worse than Christians, Jews and Manichaeans, and consider their most important duty this war against the enemy in their midst. They are called Khawārij by others but they call themselves the Muslims, or the Believers, and they call their leader the Amīr al-Mu'minīn. They keep themselves apart from the massa perditionis, according to the example of the Prophet who tore himself away from heathen Mecca. They withdraw from the hostile land, the Dār al-Ḥarb or the Dār al-Shāṭi'īn, into the Dār al-Hijra or the Dār al-Salām. This is the name they gave to the site of their headquarters, which was constantly changed.

In spite of all this they are not openly professed anarchists. The unity of the community of Believers is represented by their camp. They hold fast to the necessity of an Imām at the head of the Theocracy to lead the prayers and command the army. They simply reject the false Imāms such as 'Uthmān, 'Alī and Mu'āwiya, in order to replace them with a lawful one. The most important point is that he should be the right man. Eternal bliss depends on it. Going to Heaven or to Hell is decided by political attitudes on earth. Man appears before God under the banner for which he fought here below. According to the general Islamic view, the Imām is the *Imām* in this world and the next, in life and in death. The more that depends on him, the more difficult it is for the Khawārij to find him. He must always prove whether he be the right man or not through his actions. The moment that he commits a manifest transgression, however trivial it may seem, he is branded as a *Kāfir* (unbeliever). The Khawārij quarrel over this question of the Imām not only with other Muslims but also amongst themselves, and they split up into different sects over minor differences. Thus it is appropriate, even though formally incorrect, to accuse them of recognizing no *Imāra* ("authority", *The Kāmil*, p.555, l.18). If ideas make such pretensions, then they constantly destroy the communities which are supposed to realize them.[4]

When Muḥammad was distributing the booty from Hunayn in Jiʿrāna, he acted quite unjustly and the Tamīmite Dhū'l-Khuwayṣira approached and warned him to be fair. ʿUmar begged to be allowed to strike off the impudent fellow's head but the Prophet stopped him, saying: "Leave him: there will come forth from him people who are so zealous in praying and fasting, that your praying and fasting will seem trivial to you. They will plunge so deeply into religion that they will come out again on the other side,[5] just as a sharp arrow passes through a deer without a trace of blood or gore."[6] Naturally, the story of these premature forerunners of the Khawārij belongs to legend. Yet it is true that previously with the booty and the state treasury, Muḥammad had acted as arbitrarily as ʿUthmān and his successor and that one could attach the same blame to him on similar principles. But my prime concern is the pertinent critique of the Khawārij which is given here. Because of their increasingly extreme observance of the principles of Islam, they were led more and more beyond its tenets.

The religion of the Khawārij is certainly political: they have as their aim the divine community. But their politics are not based upon accessible goals and are perfectly barbarous: *fiat iustitia, pereat mundus*! They themselves are fully aware of this principle. They do not think of victory on earth. They are content to find death in battle. They set no store by their lives and risk their necks for the price of Paradise.[7] The background of these pious ideas forms the living conviction both of the vain-glory of the lower world and of its short duration. The hour of reckoning is at hand. Through the most extreme form of military energy, they adopt what is in fact a quite unpolitical mode of political action which is supposed to take them to Heaven. They wish to save their souls by fighting the impious community with total lack of consideration for themselves and others. They are renowned enemies of the unified community, true nonconformists and separatists. The truth is that the individual represents himself. He must be completely dedicated to the righteousness of his religio-political belief. He must strive for it with all his strength, always speak the truth (Agh; vol.XVI, p.157), and particularly be ready to prove it by his deeds. Whoever doubts his own rectitude is an unbeliever (Agh. vol.XX, p.98, p.105). But also whoever deviates from the path of righteousness by his actions is an unbeliever, especially if he claims that it could not have been avoided whatever the circumstances. (Agh.vol.XX, p.104). Whoever takes one false step has fallen off from Islam and he can only be admitted again by open repentance and an enthusiastic change of heart. The most stringent testing (miḥna) and judging of the position of belief is prescribed. Naturally, this is directed not only against one's individual person but, preferably, against others. Adiaphora (in contrast to the Muḥillūn) will not be permitted. So in fact the Khawārij are individualistic to an extreme degree, but in a very particular way. Although it is quite characteristic of them to put their belief in action and to back this up with the sword, as soon as a few like-minded people came together, they then founded theoretical heresy, or, one might say, theology. They were the first to raise religious questions which went beyond mere tradition and they debated them with their opponents. They never denied their origins in the Qur'ān readers. Without any doubt, the oldest theologians in Islam are inspired from them.[8]

1. Theoph. p.439, l.13, ed. de Boor.

2. Ṭab.II, p.184, l.8s. Agh. vol.XX, p.104, ll.17ss, p.106, ll.7,22, p.107, l.7.

3. Mushrikūn, Aḥzāb (ethnē) Shāṭi'ūn or more exactly Ahl al-Ridda.

4. The political position of the Khawārij is clarified by the opposition of the Murji'ites, which was directed not only against them but also against the Shī'a (Agh.vol.VII,p.11, l.24, p.16, ll.12ss.) and which blunted the edge of the older factions. They protested that the Khawārij only considered themselves as Muslims, that in general they always had their own rigid judgement about the position of belief of all men and so anticipated God's judgement. They thought that all those who followed a false Imām might still remain good Muslims. The question "'Alī or 'Uthmān" they left to God. They also repudiated Omayyad rule, and in the case of this denial took up a position similar to the others. They did not nominate immediately and positively one true opposing candidate for Caliph, but contented themselves in the meantime with acting on behalf of the impersonal Law. A more active representative of their cause was Ḥārith b. Surayj in Khurāsān, and their principles are expounded in a poem by Thābit Quṭna which van Vloten translated in the Journal of the DMG 1891, p.162s.

5. This explains the term Māriqūn, which is used synonymously with Khawārij. For the verb can also mean: transfodit et ab altera parte exivit (sagitta).

6. Ibn Hishām, p.844, Ṭab.I, p.1,682. Wāq. p.377. The Kāmil, p.545. Bukh.II, p.159, p.161s., p.187s., p.226s., III, p.62, p.114, p.196. IV, p.63, p.161s., p.183ss. The nickname Dhū'l-Khuwayṣira alternates with Dhū'l-Thudayya and al-Mukhdaj. All three mean the same, a man with a mutilated arm, whose hand is a mass of flesh like a woman's breast. (Wāq. p.377 to be corrected according to Ibn al-Athīr III, p.292 and al-Mas'ūdi IV, p.416.) According to The Kāmil, p.595, l.18 and others, it is supposed to have been the Tamīmite Harqūṣ b. Zuhayr

about whom Ṭab.I, p.2,541ss., p.2,955, p.3,360s. pp.3,364ss., p.3,380, p.3,382 should be consulted. But in fact he is largely anonymous. ʿAlī ordered a search for the body of Dhū'l-Thudayya on the battlefield of Nahrawān (Ṭab.I, p.3,383s.). ʿAlī had related so much about a "Mukhdaj" as being typical of the Khawārij, that a certain Nāfiʿ who was mukhdaj (that is, who had a mutilated arm) finally imagined himself to be the one referred to and acted as though this fantasy were true. (Ṭab.I, p.3,388). In verses of the Shīʿite Sayyid al-Ḥimyarī (Agh. vol.VII, p.13) the story goes that men appear at the Resurrection under five banners; four of them are evil, those of the Golden Calf, the Pharoah, the Samaritan and the Mukhdaj: the fifth and right one is that of ʿAlī. This legendary arch-Khārijite who is anonymous appears thus to be a very old notion.

7. Hence their name al-Shurāt - "the salesmen" (old Arabic, e.g. ʿUrwa b. al-Ward, III, l.2) which is found also in Theoph. p.366, l.28. Because paraboulos stands for parabolos and is derived from paraballesthai tēn psuchēn -to sacrifice one's life.

8. For further discussions of Khārijite religious and political ideas see E.A. Salem, Political Theory and Institutions of the Khawārij (Baltimore, 1956), and W.M. Watt, "Khārijite Thought in the Umayyad Period", Islam, XXXVI (1961), pp.215-231. (L)

CHAPTER 6.

The principal source for the further history of the Khawārij - in particular those from Kūfa - is first and foremost Abū Mikhnaf. The Khawārij had defected from the Shī'a in which they grew up because they were angry with 'Alī; their reason was that, after making the pact with the Syrians, he did not promptly break it and demonstrate his desire to make amends for the firm denial of their belief, i.e. their belief in the unconditional rights of Islam, as opposed to the ungodly dealings of 'Uthmān and Mu'āwiya. At first they were not implacable in their opposition to him and were persuaded to give up their camp in Ḥarūrā' and to return to his headquarters in Kūfa.[1] But he produced fresh disappointments for them and, after almost a year, a second secession took place. Although it contained by no means so many participants as the first, this made them all the more resolute. They elected their own caliph, choosing the Azdite 'Abdalla b. Wahb al-Rāsibī, who was known as the man with the camel weals, because, like James the Just, his knees were completely calloused from excessive praying.[2] Under his leadership they wanted to wage the holy war against the Unbelievers, who also included 'Alī and his supporters. They left Kūfa secretly in small groups to assemble in Nahrawān on the other side of the Tigris. Their Baṣran supporters joined them there, 500 men under the command of the Tamīmite Miṣ'ar b. Fadakī. On the way, these men encountered the distinguished 'Abdalla b. Shabbāb. They interrogated him about his position vis-à-vis 'Uthmān and 'Alī and they were not satisfied with his reply.[3] In all other respects, they had very tender consciences: one spat out a picked date because it did not belong to him, another gave back a swine which he had slain unlawfully to its Christian owner. But with a Muslim who was not a true believer, they were uncompromising. They led Ibn Shabbāb to the water and butchered him there, along with his wife who was with him. They subsequently perpetrated other similar murders.[4]

As a result, the Kūfans were up in arms. 'Alī led them against the miscreants in Nahrawān, being allegedly forced to do so. The Tamīmites Ma'qil b. Qays and Shabath b. Rib'ī (who himself had been one of the Ḥarūrites) and the Anṣārī Abū Ayyūb, Abū Qatāda and Qays b. Sa'd are quoted as the leaders of his large army. The Khawārij refused his request to hand over the murderers. They were all murderers. They wanted no peace negotiations but only death in battle against the superior power: "Do not indulge in words, prepare yourselves to appear before the face of God - this night we shall meet again in Paradise!" Then some who were reluctant to draw swords against 'Alī took themselves off to the mountains, others went over to his side or turned away and returned home to Kūfa. On the 9th Ṣafar 37 (17th July 658) they came to blows. From the original 4,000 men, only 2,800 had stayed by al-Rāsibī. The greater part of these fell with their Caliph. The wounded were taken back to Kūfa by the victors, where they were carefully nursed by their families.

This crushing victory did not make an end of the Khawārij; instead they took new life from the blood of their martyrs. Its one real effect was to make their split with the Jamā'a irreparable for all time, as wide as the rift between Kalb and Qays because of the battle of Marj Rāhiṭ. The most distinguished victim of their vengeance for Nahrawān was the Caliph 'Alī himself because the assassin was urged on by his wife Qatāmī who had lost her father and brother in that blood bath. This was a case of a Murādite avenging a Tamīmite; no tribal affair, but one concerning the party or the sect.

Ibn al-Athīr (III, pp.313ss.) mentions some of the immediate sequels to Nahrawān: Ashras b. 'Awf al-Shaybānī, who had gone with 200 men to Daskara, was killed in Rabī' II, 38/658; Hilāl b. 'Ullāfa of the Taym Ribāb and his brother Mujālid, who led more than 200 men in Māhsabadan, died in Jumādā I 38/658; Ashhab b. Bishr of the Bajīla, who had 180 men behind him, was killed at Jarjarāya on the Tigris.[5] Then Abū Maryam of the Sa'ad Tamīm ventured as far as the gates of Kūfa itself, killed one of 'Alī's captains and himself was slain in Ramaḍān 38/658. His troops consisted almost entirely of Mawālī who were the bravest and boldest of the Khawārij even then.[6]

Abū Mikhnaf in Ṭab.I, p.3,380 merely says that 500 mounted Khawārij under Farwa b. Nawfal al-Ashjaʻī escaped the slaughter at Nahrawān because they took no part at all in the battle but withdrew to Bandanijān near Daskara in Shahrazur. They were joined by Khanthara b. ʻUbayda al-Muḥāribī, who was gravely wounded at Ṣiffīn (pp.3,309s.). They had no desire to fight against ʻAlī and their Kūfan bretheren. After his death, according to Bakkā'ī (on the authority of ʻAwāna , Ṭab.II, p.10), they fought all the more energetically against Muʻāwiya. When Muʻāwiya had occupied Iraq and was encamped at Nukhayla near Kūfa, they attacked him and destroyed a part of his army. Then he warned the Kūfans about how the peace would be disrupted if they did not get rid of these brazen types. The Kūfans obeyed him and killed the Khawārij, who realized too late how their brothers who died at Nahrawān had been in the right. Farwa b. Nawfal, however, was kept at home by relatives before the battle took place.[7,8]

After the defeat of al-Rāsibī, the Khawārij chose another Caliph from Kūfa, when Mughīra had become governor. This was Mustawrid b. ʻUllāfa of the Taym Ribāb, whose brothers Hilāl and Mujālid, according to Ibn al-Athīr, had been martyred in the fighting after Nahrawān. Abū Mikhnaf's story is essentially that of two eye witnesses, separated from him by only one intermediary authority. He has so harmonized the two accounts that they have completely merged and form a unified whole, although they derive from opposite camps. One of the witnesses is a Khārijite, ʻAbdalla b. ʻUqba al-Ghanawī, who, as a fairly young man played quite an important part in the affair and who later deserted the faction. He is an attractive personality and his report gives a clear picture of these earliest Khawārij and so is very informative, although it concerns only an episodic putsch.

Ḥayyān b. Ẓubyān al-Sulamī belonged to the Khārijite wounded at Nahrawān whom ʻAlī had allowed to return to Kūfa. After about a month he left Kūfa and went to Rayy with some ten companions. But on hearing the news of ʻAlī's murder "at the hands of our brother of Murād", they very gladly left their hiding place and returned to Kūfa to seek revenge for Nahrawān. They openly proclaimed their readiness to act for the neglected Sunna against the impious regents and, even if they had no success, at least their souls would find favour in God's eyes. That took place in the time of Ḥasan b. ʿAlī. During Muʿāwiya's reign, Mughīra b. Shuʿba became Governor of Kūfa. He did not interfere with those who had political grievances, provided that they did not translate their words into actions. "God has decreed that you will always have inner strife, and hereafter it depends not on me but on Him to settle the questions which divide you." On this principle he also turned a blind eye to the Khawārij. They celebrated the memory of the martyrs of Nahrawān and blamed themselves for their inactivity. They declared that the war against the Ahl al-Qibla - i.e. against the Catholic Muslims - was their divine mission. They had regular meetings in the house of Ḥayyān b. Ẓubyān. Amongst them were two others of the wounded who had been pardoned, one a Ṭāʾī, Muʿādh b. Juwayn, a male cousin of Zayd b. Ḥusayn who died at Nahrawān, and the other, the Tamīmite Mustawrid - their most distinguished man. Neither was jealous of the other and each was willing to recognize the other as leader. Finally, as the eldest, Mustawrid received the oath of allegiance. This took place in Jumādā II and was the signal to attack. On the first of Shaʿbān, 43/663, they decided to move out.[9] But Mughīra got wind of this and one day had a group of some twenty people arrested at Ḥayyān's house; his wife had just time to conceal their swords under the carpet. Because Mughīra was not satisfied with the excuse of those arrested, that they were simply reciting the Qurʾān with Ḥayyān, he kept them in prison for almost a year.[10] Taking this as a warning, Mustawrid left Kūfa and went to the neighbouring Christian city of Ḥīra, to a compound near the castle of the ʿAdasites. His companions came with him and prepared to march out. They were surprised there by Ḥajjār b. Abjar, a noble Bakrite of Christian origin.[11] Although he promised not to betray them, and kept his word, they nevertheless abandoned this position and took shelter in Kūfa. Mustawrid along with six or seven companions found shelter with the ʿAbd al-Qaysite Sulaym b. Mahduj, who was related to him by marriage but was no Khārijite.

The governor, Mughīra, had heard several rumours without knowing anything more precise. On the occasion of the next Friday prayer, he explained from the Minbar that he wished to cause no violence and did not want to involve innocent people in the guilt of a few trouble-makers. Nevertheless, he had to ask the reasonable ones to restrain their unreasonable members whose names he did not know. Each tribal leader summoned his tribesmen and bound them on oath to denounce anyone they knew. Ṣaʿṣaʿa b. Ṣuhan, did the same with the ʿAbd al-Qays. He reproached them by saying that they had always been true Companions of Muḥammad and ʿAlī and therefore were enemies of the Khawārij. They had no reason to risk a conflict with authority because of them and they must not guarantee them any shelter. All those present showed their enthusiasm for this, only Sulaym b. Mahduj remained silent. He was unwilling to drive out the Khawārij who had fled to him, but also did not wish to get into trouble with them. Mustawrid helped him out of his dilemma by deciding to withdraw of his own accord. He asked his men to leave their quarters in little groups and to assemble in the town of Sura. This they did and from there they went on further to Ṣarāt. They numbered altogether three hundred men.

When the governor became aware of this, he summoned the leaders of the tribes and asked which of them was willing to march against the rebels. Inclined to Shīʿism as they were, they all burned with zeal. Ṣaʿṣaʿa b. Ṣuhan of the ʿAbd al-Qays was especially devoted and proposed himself, but Mughīra snubbed him because he used to slander ʿUthmān and sing ʿAlī's praises in public and private. Mughīra was so much more in favour of the Tamīmite Maʿqil b. Qays and gave him 3,000 men chosen from the most zealous Shīʿites.

According to Abū Mikhnaf, the former Khārijite ʿAbdalla b. ʿUqba al-Ghanawī relates the following story: "When we were all together in Ṣarāt, we went from there towards Behrasir[12] to cross the Tigris at that point. But Simāk b. ʿUbayd al-ʿAbsī, the governor of Madāʾin, destroyed the pontoon bridges and prevented us from crossing. Mustawrid dictated a letter to me for him: 'We are displeased at the unrighteousness of the judges' verdict, the non-observance of the penal law and the arbitrary distribution of the state revenue. We demand that you accept as the rule of conduct the Book of God, the example of the Prophet and the rule of Abū Bakr and ʿUmar, and also that you abandon the causes of ʿUthmān and ʿAlī who have introduced <u>bidʿa</u> into religion and have denied the Holy Book. If you will not do this, we have done all we can and declare war on you.' Then I myself had to carry over this letter. The task was a painful one for me. On hearing Mustawrid's order, I could have thrown myself into the Tigris. I was unskilled in affairs and also feared that Simāk would keep me prisoner, so that I would be unable to take part in the battle. However, Mustawrid told me that as an envoy I was safe from attack, so I went off with the letter, over a ford and through the stream. When I came to the place, I was confused by the glances directed towards me. Then, when some ten men approached in order to examine me, I drew my sword with the words: 'I am the envoy of Mustawrid, the Prince of the Believers.' They calmed me down and took me to Simāk; his companions surrounded me and held my arm and my sword hilt fast. He read the letter and said: 'I would not have believed of the smooth, meek Mustawrid that he draws his sword against Muslims, asks me to abandon ʿAlī and ʿUthmān and to recognize him as leader! My son, tell your master to change his mind and to turn again to the community of Muslims. I will arrange his safe conduct with Mug͟hīra, who is quite prepared to pardon and forgive.' I was at that time heart and soul a K͟hārijite and answered: 'We strive only for safe conduct with God on the Day of Resurrection!' He turned to his followers and said: 'They have chosen this youth and mumbled Qur'ān phrases to him, pretending to be contrite and to weep, and have led him astray with their pious sentimentality.' I replied: 'I have not come in order to quarrel with him and to listen to his talk. He should tell me whether or not he accepts what is in the letter, so that I may inform my master.' He was amazed that I, a mere boy, should address such words to a man who was older than my father and he dismissed me, saying: 'My son, when the cavalrymen surround you and point the lances towards you, then you will wish that you were with your mother!' Thereupon I turned back and brought the news to Mustawrid."

Mustawrid was quite happy to take the advice to resist the Kūfans in Behrasir and to gain martyrdom, for this world meant no more to him than his bootlace. But he preferred to exhaust and split up the pursuers by means of forays in different directions. He went from the Tigris to a position opposite Jarjarāya and there crossed the river into the land of Jūkhā, until he reached Madhār which was already part of Baṣran territory.[13] Three days later, when the Kūfans came via Sura and Kutha to Behrasir, they were disappointed not to find the Khawārij there any more and that they had to prepare themselves for a long weary pursuit. Their leader Ma'qil b. Qays sent Abū Rawāgh al-Shākirī with 300 cavalry to pursue them and to hold them. He found them at Madhār and, although unable to withstand their attack, he still did not leave them until Ma'qil followed with the main army.[14] At sunset there ensued a furious battle. The Khawārij were driven back by the superior forces into the houses of Madhār. When they heard that almost 3,000 Baṣran Shī'ites, mostly from the Rabī'a tribes, were on the point of arriving under the command of Sharīk b. al-A'war al-Ḥārithī,[15] and that they were already in the neighbourhood, they went off secretly by night and returned to Kūfan territory beyond Jarjarāya by way of a detour. They were sure that the Baṣrans would not follow them there. Nor were they deceived in their expectation: the Baṣrans would not allow their leader to move to help the Kūfans for they had more pressing business to attend to at home. They did not wish to resemble a mother who neglects her own children for the sake of strange ones. Again, Ma'qil sent Abū Rawāgh forward with 600 cavalry to stick to the heels of the Khawārij. It was already early in the morning when he found them at Jarjarāya. Because they were unable to shake him off quickly, they broke off and went back over the Tigris to Sabāt,[16] and camped there on the bank of the Nahr Malik which lay in the direction of Kūfa. Abū Rawāgh came after them and pitched camp on the opposite bank. Then Mustawrid took a quick decision. While misleading Abū Rawāgh, he turned against Ma'qil himself who had followed with the main Kūfan army and was camped at Daylamayya, three parasangs below Behrasir. Ma'qil was taken by surprise and his army was scattered. Only 300 men stayed by him; they knelt down with outstretched lances and defended themselves desperately against the attackers. The Khawārij were close to victory when suddenly Abū Rawāgh appeared and took them in the rear. The result was that they were almost all killed, after they had doubtless sold their lives dearly. Mustawrid speared Ma'qil through the back with his lance and Ma'qil split his head open with his sword. 'Abdalla b. 'Uqba, known to us as the youthful messenger to Simāk, saved himself on a captured horse and reached Kūfa, bringing with him the first report of the outcome of the battle. As a reward, he was pardoned. Moreover, Mughīra would undoubtedly have pardoned all the Khawārij if they had surrendered to him.

For many years the Kūfan Khawārij remained calm, until they again chose a Caliph. That was always the signal for the resumption of action against the Jamā'a. The authority for Abū Mikhnaf's account is once again 'Abdalla b. 'Uqba al Ghanawī. The revolt took place in the year 58-9/677-8 when Ibn Umm Ḥakam al-Thaqafī was Governor in Kūfa. It began amongst all those who had not been able to share in Mustawrid's attempted coup, as they sat behind lock and key. They felt bitter regret about all their inactivity hitherto: "God has given us hearts and minds to protest against unrighteousness and to fight against transgressors. Our excuse with God can only lie in death." Ḥayyān b. Ẓubyān al-Sulamī was chosen as Caliph. His old companion Mu'ādh b. Juwayn was the first to pay the oath of allegiance to him. He proposed going to Ḥulwān to assemble all the like-minded supporters between Kūfa and Rayy.[17] However, Ḥayyān disagreed, saying: "They will not leave you enough time for that; we shall die in the holy battle here, for we are not even a hundred men and could not hope to achieve anything." Although some opposed him, saying that this was to no purpose, but simply removed a thorn from the flesh of his enemies, he stood by his point of view and the others were unwilling to contradict him. But they did not wish to attack inside Kūfa itself, for there they ran the risk of being injured by rocks thrown from the roof-tops by women and children; instead they went nearby to Banaqiya and stood with their backs against the houses there so that they had the enemy in front of them. As they desired, they were all slain, in Rabī' I, 59.[18]

---

1. 'Alī visited the secessionists at Ḥarūrā'. In the course of trying to satisfy their scruples, he may have given them reason to expect that he would repudiate the agreement to arbitrate. E.I. (new edition), III, pp.235-36; Vaglieri, Il conflitto 'Alī-Mu'āwiya, pp.42-47. (L)

2. Eusebius of Caesarea (c.260-340) Historia Ecclesiastica, II, p.23. (James the Just, or Saint James, was so called for his pious observance of Jewish Law. Ed.)

3. According to another statement, they were angry with him because he spread the view that the Prophet had said that one should not participate actively in civil wars, but rather allow oneself to be slaughtered than to shed Muslim blood.

4. The evidence from Khārijite sources suggests that the Khārijites who withdrew to Nahrawān had no hostile intentions. They simply refused to accept ʿAlī as Caliph and were waiting out the crisis. Vaglieri, Il conflitto ʿAlī-Muʿāwiya, pp.60-69. (L)

5. Between the revolt of Ashhab and Abū Maryam, Ibn al-Athīr gives another episode - the revolt of Saʿīd b. Qufl al Taymī of Taym-Allah, of Thaʿlaba, with 200 men. W.M. Watt, "Khārijite Thought", p.215 and Ibn al-Athīr, The Kāmil, III p.314, 1.8s. (L)

6. cf. Yaʿqūbī, II, p.262.

7. The Kāmil (of al-Mubarrad) distinguishes between two Khārijite battles at Nukhayla - (i) against ʿAlī, with Mustawrid as their leader (p.576s., cf. p.548); (ii) against Muʿāwiya, with Ḥawthara al-Asadī as their leader (p.577s.) The occurrence here of Mustawrid's name is premature and Ḥawthara al-Asadī should read Khanthara al-Muḥāribī. The people of Nukhayla (i) who fought against ʿAlī are supposed to have been those who had not wished to oppose him at Nahrawān but it is much more likely that at Nukhayla (i) they wished to oppose Muʿāwiya rather than ʿAlī. Indeed Yāqūt (II, p.153) includes the verses which, according to The Kāmil p.577, refer to Nukhayla (i) rather than to Nukhayla (ii), with much greater justification because it can scarcely be believed of ʿAlī that he had the severed heads of the Khawārij brought to him in heaps. Consequently, there is in fact no difference between Nukhayla (i) and (ii). If Sayyid al-Ḥimyarī (The Kāmil, p.577) considers the battle in that place as

being waged against 'Alī, then he would in fact be leading the Kūfans against the Shī'a; they, the Kūfans, certainly marched against the Khawārij in obedience to Mu'āwiya's orders but they surely did not do so unwillingly.

8. The list of Khārijite uprisings may be expanded to include 'Abdalla b. Abī'l-Hawsā al-Ṭā'ī, Mu'ayn b. 'Abdalla al-Muḥāribī and Abū Laylā. See Watt, Khārijite Thought, p.216. (L)

9. Ṭab.II, p.21. If the date of the attack occurred in the year 43/663, then without doubt the oath of allegiance also took place in this year and not, as it appears according to Ṭabarī, in the previous year. An intervening gap of 14 months cannot have been contemplated right from the outset. On the other hand, it is possible that because of the attendant obstacles, the date of the attack was postponed. Then perhaps the year 43/663 would be the date of the actual attack, whilst originally it had been agreed on for 42/662. The year 43 began on 15th April, 663. cf. Ya'qūbī, II, p.262.

10. cf. also in Ṭab.II, p.36, the verses of Mu'ādh who was imprisoned with them, where he urges the other party members to break out of the territory of the impious ones, deploring the fact that he could not go with them.

11. Ṭab.I, p.3,460. II, p.235. II, pp.29-30.

12. Opposite Madā'in (Ctesiphon); the Greek Selucia. In Theophanes, p.323, l.18, (de Boor) Guedesir, like Adesir, for Ardeshir. c.f. Noeldeke's Ṭabarī, p.10, n.3. (Geschichte der Perser und Araber zur Zeit der Sasaniden, Leiden 1879).

13. It seems, therefore, that Madhār, an important position, lay on the left bank of the Tigris, like Jarjarāya.

14. He was advised to own himself defeated and to vacate the field, for God was not ashamed of the Truth. But nolebat sibi verum confiteri - in the words of Trimalchio. (The quotation is from Cena Trimalchionis, ch.26-78 of Petronius' Satyricon.)

15. He was a zealous Shīʿite. (Ṭab.I, p.3,417, II, pp.196, 241-49.)

16. One of the cities opposite Ctesiphon, like Behrasir.

17. This was the border city of Kūfan territory.

18. Ibn Umm Ḥakam took up office in 58/677 and left it in the year 59. The tragedy of Banaqiya occurred in his final year. That can only mean the second year of the Hijra when he lived in Kūfa; for his term of office lasted scarcely a year. Therefore Rabīʿ I 59 = January 679.

CHAPTER 7.

That was the end of the Kūfan Khawārij. They were people of deep conviction, much nobler than the Jewish Zealots and no worse than Christian heretics and saints, because they were men of action who found martyrdom not upon the scaffold but upon the battlefield. To judge them from the secular viewpoint of modern culture would be unfair. Henceforth the Shī'a reigned in Kūfa without any rivals; the Khawārij were extinct there. They now became all the more active in Baṣra. At first, Ṭabarī gives only the briefest résumé of the Khawārij in Baṣra and in II, p.390, he presumes knowledge of events previously related which he had in fact not related at all. His version can be completed from that found in Ibn al-Athīr, while at this stage it would be better to disregard the account which occurs in The Kāmil.

Already, in the year 41/661, the Khārijites Sahm b. Ghālib of Tamīm and al-Khatīm of Bāhila had revolted in Baṣra with 70 men; they killed a Muslim whom they captured on the bridge over the Tigris. The Governor, Ibn 'Āmir, forced them to surrender but then pardoned them. (Ṭab.II, pp.15s. Ibn al-Athīr III, pp.350s.) When Ziyād b. Abīhi became Governor, Sahm could no longer rely on being left in peace, so he went to Ahwāz and raised a rebellion. Again he killed a Muslim who refused to deny his faith, whilst he allowed others to escape who passed themselves off as Jews. Finally, he ventured as far as Baṣra but there was abandoned by his companions and obliged to hide. Once again he hoped to be pardoned but, in the year 46/666, Ziyād had him killed and strung up outside the door of his house. Khatīm also tried to make a move but was banished by Ziyād to Baḥrayn. However, he soon was allowed to return home on condition that he did not leave his house at night. But he did not keep to this and was duly reported by his tribal chieftain, Muslim b. 'Amr al-Bāhilī, the father of the famous Qutayba. He was then executed. (Ṭab.II, p.83;

Ibn al-Athīr III, p.351, p.379). A third and fairly similar episode took place in the year 50/670. Qārib of Azd (Iyād, The Kāmil, p.677, l.11) and Zahhāf of Ṭayyi, both cousins, went out one night with 70 followers, killed one of the Ḍubayʿa and then scattered. But Qārib did not return alive. After this event, Ziyād (and his lieutenant Samura b. Jundab) hardened their approach to the Khawārij and forced the Baṣrans to get rid of them (Ṭab.II, p.91). He is supposed to have had many thousands of them killed and imprisoned (Ṭab.II, p.459). However, such high figures should not be believed. There is no real question of cruelty against the Khawārij on the part of Ziyād. He was only doing his duty, imposed upon him by the Qur'ān itself. (The Kāmil p.594). He treated murderer as murderer. These Baṣran Khawārij had much of the brigand and the assassin about them. The anarchy which reigned then in Baṣra, as opposed to Kūfa[1], was exactly the right environment for them and they could not be surprised if they received the same treatment along with all other trouble makers at the hands of the police. The nobler members of the faction wanted nothing to do with this business; Abū Bilāl cursed it and so vindicated the Governor.

The chief persecutor of the Khawārij in Baṣra is not Ziyād but his son ʿUbaydalla, who became Governor there in the year 55/674. At first, he acted mildly towards them and freed them from prison.[2] But when the anticipated effect did not come about, he changed his tune. He got hold of a band led by a certain Jidār and incited them to fight with each other. If a man had killed one of the others, he would be set free. The ʿAbdalqaysite Ṭawwāf was one of those who had killed their friends and thereby gained freedom. As a result of these actions, bitter reproaches were levelled against him and others in the same category, and so they tried to expiate their guilt through active repentance. They offered the relatives of those whom they had killed first money, and then their own blood, but in vain. So they decided, according to Sūra XVI, 111, to make good their having yielded to temptation by renewed, reckless effort and to venture to oppose ʿUbaydalla. There were 70 men, all from the tribes of ʿAbd al-Qays. They had to make a premature start because they were betrayed and were slain by the Governor's Bukhāran bodyguard on the occasion of the Fiṭr in the year 58, that is on the 27th July, 678. (Ibn al-Athīr III, p.427).[3]

After this ʿUbaydalla proceeded against the Khawārij with harsh preventive measures. He imprisoned on mere suspicion those who seemed dangerous, something which his father had never done. (The Kāmil, p.594). The highest reputation amongst the Baṣran Khawārij belonged to Abū Bilāl Mirdās b. Udayya of Tamīm, who has already been mentioned. He disapproved of the participation of women in battle[4] and condemned the Istiʿrāḍ, that is the indiscriminate killing of all non-Khārijite Muslims who came their way. ʿUbaydalla put him into prison along with the others but he obtained permission from the jailor to visit his family at night. One evening, one of his friends was informed that the imprisoned Khawārij were to be executed on the following morning and he announced this in the house of Abū Bilāl without knowing that he was present. Nevertheless, according to his promise Abū Bilāl returned to prison early in the morning. The jailor was much moved by that and informed ʿUbaydalla whose attendant he had been, and so was able to obtain freedom for the noble man, whilst the others had to suffer death. ʿUmar b. Shabba, according to Ṭab.II, p.186s., tells this well-known story which, in this version, presents the governor in an honourable light, and was therefore later amended.

Abū Bilāl's brother, ʿUrwa b. Udayya, who twenty years earlier is supposed to have first raised the shout of the Taḥkīm at Ṣiffīn, did not escape so easily. He had chosen the occasion of a race when ʿUbaydalla appeared in public as a good opportunity to approach him and charge him with five mortal sins which he had committed. The governor took this act as a prelude to revolt and, terrified, he left the arena. The other in turn was afraid at the reaction caused by his words and went into hiding, but he was discovered and cruelly put to death, his daughter along with him. He died with the words: "You have spoiled this world for me and I have spoiled the next for you."[5] A similar fate befell a zealous woman called Bathjāʾ.[6] She made inflammatory speeches about ʿUbaydalla and his tyranny. She was warned of his hostile intentions towards her but she refused to hide from him, so as not to bring others into trouble. She allowed herself to be arrested and met a martyr's death in the market-place of Baṣra.[7]

The execution of this woman, which he witnessed, made an even deeper impression on Abū Bilāl than did the death of his brother. He could take no more; he could no longer look on. In the year 60/679, he went to Ahwāz with 40 followers, for he did not believe it possible to live under this régime in Baṣra. He harmed nobody, only taking as much as he thought he ought to claim from the taxes, as a pension for himself and his followers. He merely defended himself against aggressors and did so with outstanding success. At Asak, between Ramhurmuz and Arjān, with his forty men, he put to flight a government army numbering 2,000; the numbers were already quoted in contemporary verses.[8] But in the year 61/680, he was defeated by a bigger army under the Tamīmite ʿAbbād b. Ashdar; none of his men escaped. When the victor returned home, as he was about to ride into the citadel, four men approached and told him of their business: "One of our brothers has been murdered; we have taken our grievance to the Amīr but he sent us away. What must we do?" He replied: "Kill the murderer yourselves, God curse him!" Then they shouted out the Taḥkīm, fell upon him and slew him together with his little son who sat behind him on the crupper. They were Khārijites led by ʿAbīda b. Hilāl.[9]

---

1. Ṭab.II, pp.73ss., p.88.

2. The Kāmil, p.524. (See also Anon. Ahlw, p.79, 1.6, though this is hardly an appropriate reference.) The Kāmil, p.610, 1.1.

3. Here may be added the revolts of Ziyād b. Kharrāsh al-ʿIjlī, Muʿādh b. Juwayn al-Ṭāʾī and Ṭawwāf b. Ghallāq. See Watt, Khārijite Thought, p.216. (L)

4. The zeal of the women amongst the Khārijites is often cited. Particularly famous is Umm Ḥakīm who fought under Qaṭarī. She strove for martyrdom in battle: "I no longer wish to wash and anoint my head; is there none then who will relieve me of this burden?" (Agh. vol.VI, pp.6s.) It is alleged that Ibn Ziyād tried to cool down the zeal for martyrdom amongst women by exposing their naked corpses. (The Kāmil, p.582) This method, as Plutarch reports, is

supposed to have been used to good effect already many centuries earlier against a mania for suicide amongst the young women of Miletus.

5. Ṭab.II, p.185s., according to Wahb b. Jarīr, who also wrote a book on certain Khārijites. (Agh. I, p.11, l.28).

6. The name is written like this in Ibn al-Athīr III, p.428s. In The Kāmil she is called Baljā.

7. Another similar story occurs in The Kāmil, p.602 l.15 - p.604, l.7.

8. The leader of the government army at Asak was, according to Wahb b. Jarīr in Ṭab.II, p.187, the Tamīmite Ibn Ḥiṣn; but according to Abū Mikhnaf in Ṭab.II, p.390, it was the Kilābite Aslam b. Zurʿa; so also according to The Kāmil, p.587, p.604 and Dīnawarī. cf. Ibn al-Athīr, III, p.429, l.19.

9. Ṭab.II, p.187, p.391, Ibn al-Athīr III, pp.428ss The Kāmil, pp.585ss. Ibn Ziyād is supposed to have said (The Kāmil, p.604, l.2): "As often as I have one of them killed, they kill one of my agents." Names of the prominent Baṣran Khārijites are given in The Kāmil and in the verses in Ibn al-Athīr, III, p.428.

CHAPTER 8.

The war-cry of ʿAbīda, who afterwards became notorious, was: "I follow the religion of Abū Bilāl." (The Kāmil, p.679, l.12.) Abū Bilāl was the real saint of the Baṣran Khawārij, although they did not emulate his mild ways. His martyrdom brought their anger to a peak but they could do nothing in Baṣra so long as ʿUbaydalla b. Ziyād remained firmly in the saddle. Things only changed during the upheavals which began with the death of the Caliph Yazīd I. Abū Mikhnaf, according to Ṭabarī, II, pp.513-520, gives the following account of this. ʿUbaydalla knew how to keep order in Baṣra.[1] In order to escape his pursuit, after the death of Abū Bilāl, the Khawārij went from Baṣra to Mekka and helped Ibn Zubayr against the Syrians. But after the death of Yazīd I and the retreat of the Syrians, the difference between their political standpoint and that of Ibn Zubayr became apparent,[2] so they left Mekka. The Bakrites Abū Talūt, Abū Fudayk and Ibn Aswad went to Yamāma and occupied that area. The Tamīmites Nāfiʿ b. Azraq,[3,4] ʿAbdalla b. Ṣaffār, ʿAbdalla b. Ibāḍ, Ḥanẓala b. Baihas, ʿAbdalla, ʿUbaydalla and Zubayr[5] from the Māhūz family, went to Baṣra. The flight of ʿUbaydalla and the tribal strife in Baṣra provided the Khawārij with some relief and the prisoners broke free. Ibn Azraq was at the head of a band of 300 men and went with them to Ahwaz.[6] After the Baṣrans were united once more with the Qurayshite Bābba as their Āmir, they all acted together against the remaining Khawārij in the city and forced them to flee to join Ibn Azraq. Only a few remained behind with Ibn Ṣaffār and Ibn Ibāḍ. They thus remained apart from Ibn Azraq, who stressed the principle that a true Muslim must not stay with idolaters but should completely abandon their community. However, Ibn Ṣaffār and Ibn Ibāḍ were also not quite in agreement with each other. Ibn Azraq had the most followers. He advanced to a position close by the bridge of Baṣra. The governor Bābba sent the Qurayshite Muslim b. ʿUbays against him.[7]

According to other authorities followed by Brünnow (p.38), it was ʿUbaydalla himself who let the Khawārij out of prison, as a favour to the Baṣrans, and it is said that they joined forces with the Tamīmites against the Azdites in the Baṣran tribal feuds. But this casts an entirely false light on the position of the Baṣrans vis à vis the Khawārij. The Baṣrans were extremely hostile to them; nor were the Tamīmites any exception to this, in spite of Brünnow's opinion. In fact the Khawārij did not help the Tamīmites against the Azdites but the Asāwira did so.[8] If ʿUbaydalla had freed the Khārijite prisoners, this would have been no favour to the Baṣrans and could indeed have done them harm. Abū Mikhnaf's assertion is much more likely - namely that they broke loose (rather than were freed).[9]

The principal objective of Abū Mikhnaf is to tell the story of the fragmentation of the Khawārij. The names which he quotes are (with the exception of the three grandchildren of Māhūz) names of the founders of parties or sects: the Azāriqa stem from Ibn Azraq, the Ṣufriyya from Ibn Ṣaffār, the Ibāḍiyya from Ibn Ibāḍ, the Bayhasiyya from Ibn Bayhas. (Ṭab.II,p.1,897, 1.20). However he does not explain the origins of the fragmentation and this is equally the case with other authorities, (e.g. The Kāmil, p.604, ll.7-12). The four sects at given moments suddenly appear on the scene. They were considered as theological schools by later historians of dogma. According to Abū Mikhnaf and also according to Madāʾinī (in The Kāmil and in Anon. Ahlwardt), a common opposition against Ibn Azraq emerges, to the effect that his apparent extremism and perhaps also the jealousy of the others, became the origin of the disagreements. He must have made the greatest impression in his time, even though he did not become prominent before the year 64/683 and was already dead by the year 65/684. According to The Kāmil, p.604s., Abū Wāziʿ al-Rāsibī was responsible for rousing him from his hitherto peaceful state; he stirred him into action and had words replaced by swords. In order to demonstrate what he should do, Abū Wazīʿ bought a sword from a sword-smith and struck Ibn Azraq with it, because he was speaking ill of the Khawārij; then he cut himself a bloody path through the terrified people, who scattered in all directions. He was finally killed in the quarter of the Banū Yashkūr,[10] and to their dismay was buried there, for they feared that his grave would become a shrine for his devotees. This fine example made an Khārijī, or a Shārī, of Nāfi‘ , whilst previously he had been a qā‘id.[11]

Ever since then his foremost principle was that in no circumstances should one remain in the midst of the Unbelievers; one must emigrate (to a Dār al-Hijra) and sell one's life to God in the struggle against them. All those Khawārij who remained in Baṣra defected from him because of that. Certainly they also wished to rebel sometime, but on a suitable and not an unsuitable occasion. The difference of opinion turned merely on the question of the opportunity. This was not exactly new, for a minority of active members always arose out of a wider circle of inactive people. From time to time the open fire blazed forth from the ashes in which the coals were still warm. But now the difference of opinion became particularly prominent. In addition, there arose similar points of dispute on which Ibn Azraq always adopted the most extreme position. He upheld the Isti‘rāḍ which was an old practice amongst the Baṣran Khawārij but which was rejected by Abū Bilāl. He extended the break with the Jamā‘a to families and inheritance groups. He submitted the Muhājira, i.e. the new recruits to the party, to a severe inquisition and disregarded conversion according to Taqiya, that is because of fear and without inner conviction.[12] The others were more lenient on these points, although to different degrees which can scarcely be distinguished. The principal point of conflict always remained, namely that they allowed themselves to remain in a temporary state of latent hostility and were not always in open conflict with the unbelieving community. Yet, whenever they did undertake any action, they proved to be no less reckless than the Azāriqa.

Those sects which originated in the opposition to Ibn Azraq, later spread from Baṣra throughout the Khawārij within the total area of Islam. But there is another Khārijite sect which, because of its short existence and restricted locality, is usually not considered with the others. That is the Najadāt from the Arab territory of Yamāma, which belonged to Baṣra. They consisted of Bakrites who lived there and, in particular, the defiant peasants of Ḥanīfa. They derived their name from Najdā b. ‘Āmir al-Ḥanafī. He was the one who led the Khawārij to assist Ibn Zubayr in Mecca, (Ṭab.II, p.401s., p.425,

1.14). After the siege of Mecca was raised, he did
not join those who returned home to Yamāma but went
with Ibn Azraq, his tribesman, to Baṣra in the year
64/683. He soon left him, however, as he could not
agree with him and was also in the shadow of the
other's reputation. He then returned to Yamāma. 13
We have two concurring accounts about his activities:
one containing the essential points derives from
Madā'inī, then one finds a more detailed version in
Anon. Ahlwardt, pp.125ss., and a shorter one in Ibn
al-Athīr, IV, p.165ss.

The Khawārij of Yamāma had chosen Abū Talūt as
their leader on the express condition that he should
rule only until they found a better candidate. In
the year 65/684 (*Anon*. p.127), he settled down in
Khadārim, one of the large estates in Yamāma occupied by Mu'āwiya which was cultivated by 4,000
slaves. But the following year he was forced to
withdraw by Najdā who had received the oath of
allegiance as Caliph in the year 66/685 (Ibn al-
Athīr, p.166).[14] The slaves of Khadārim had been
distributed as booty but Najdā was responsible for
allowing them, at the party's cost, to cultivate the
land again as a community, as had previously been
the case. At Jabala he captured a caravan coming
from Baṣra which was destined for Ibn Zubayr in
Mecca (*Anon*. p.127). In Dhū 'l-Majāz he attacked
the clan of 'Āmir b. Ṣa'ṣa'a and, after a bloody
battle, robbed them of the store of corn and dates
which they had pillaged from the market: many verses
refer to the event and the impression which it created (*Anon*. pp.128-31). With these raids he went
around subduing the Arab territories (i.e. exacting
tribute from them), in particular, the fertile
coastal strips in the North East and South West, just
as Muḥammad in Medīna once did. He was helped by
the weakness of the régime of Ibn Zubayr. 'Abd al-
Malik feigned friendliness towards him and agreed to
endorse his control over the province of Yamāma if
he in turn would give him his support (*Anon*. p.143).
But Najdā did not allow himself to be tempted in this
way and, instead, proceeded as far as he could.
Leaving a governor in Yamāma, he himself went to
Baḥrayn[15] in the year 67/686 (*Anon*. p.131). He won
over the Azdites, attacked the 'Abd al-Qays at Qaṭīf
and settled down in the city. In order to expel
him from Qaṭīf, Ḥamza b. Zubayr b. 'Abdalla, who 16
represented his father in Baṣra, sent that same year
14,000 Baṣrans led by 'Abdalla b. 'Umair al-Laythī.

But Najdā attacked him, put them to flight and captured the camp. Farazdaq publicly satirized those who fled in verses full of reproach (Anon. p.134). Then on Najdā's orders, ʻAtiya b. Aswad al-Ḥanafī subjugated ʻUmān but the reigning dynasty there, the Banū Jalanda, seized it from him again. He severed relations with Najdā, crossed the Persian Gulf and settled down in Kirmān. Then he had to flee to Sijistān pursued by Muhallab, and then even further to Sind and was finally killed at Qandebīl.[17] Meanwhile, Najdā himself extended his rule over northern Baḥrayn (Kātzima) and forced the Tamīm to pay taxes to him. Then he went from Yamāma to the other regions of Western Arabia and subjugated part of Yemen, with its capital Ṣanʻā; by means of his captain Abū Fudayk, he also conquered the bordering state of Ḥaḍramaut in the year 68/687. At the end of the year, he appeared at the Meccan festival with his army of 860 men and there, in friendly circumstances, four different factions under different banners participated in the procession from ʻArafa.[18] He gave up his intention to attack Medīna when he heard that ʻAbdalla b. ʻUmar was arming against him. Like all the Khawārij, he had the greatest veneration for the father of this man, the Caliph ʻUmar I. Thus he is supposed to have asked ʻUmar's son for written instructions on all manner of questions. These matters were too subtle for ʻAbdalla and he left the answers to Ibn ʻAbbās who was greatly surprised that a man who did not shrink from shedding streams of Muslim blood should have such scruples in apparently minor affairs. We find Najdā again in Ṭā'if, where the government representative willingly allowed himself to be subdued, and again he appears further south in Tabāla. He organized the administration of that area and established his officials.[19] Then he turned back to Baḥrayn. Whilst he did not wish to bear arms against the holy cities of Mecca and Medīna, he did not hesitate to blockade their supplies from Baḥrayn and Yamāma until Ibn ʻAbbās, comparing his conduct to that of Muḥammad, proved to him that this was unlawful.

Najdā was not far from extending his hegemony over the whole of Arabia: Ibn Zubayr could do little about it. But his power was weakened by internal quarrels and it eventually broke down altogether. The Khawārij could not endure any authority for long. Naturally, they raised opposition on "religious grounds", as they put it. He had given some troops more pay than others and, as a result, the above-mentioned ʿAtiya b. Aswad had already fallen foul of him, for he implied that Najdā had a secret agreement with ʿAbd al-Malik. He had also saved a captured granddaughter of the Caliph ʿUthmān from the fate which captive women tended to suffer. This was again an offence against Divine Law from human motives; it was even alleged that it had been done for fear of the menace of Ibn Zubayr, (Anon. p.138, 1.6. Ibn al-Athīr, p.168, 1.13). He committed another atrocity in that he did not wish to get rid of a competent man who had drunk wine. The longer it went on, the more numerous and louder were the protests. He promised to repent and to improve but the trouble makers always found new motives. Finally, they set up another Amīr in opposition to him. First, their choice fell upon a Mawlā, the date-merchant Thābit but they soon found they would have to have a pure Arab at their head and ordered the Mawlā to choose a suitable man.[20] He chose Abū Fudayk who took the oath of allegiance. Najdā hid from him in one of the villages of Hajar and, when he was betrayed there, he hid amongst his maternal relatives of the Tamīm. He had intended to go to ʿAbd al-Malik (to Kūfa?) but his enemies forestalled him. He was stopped and slain, after spurning a swift horse offered to him for his escape. That happened, according to Ṭabarī, p.829, in the year 72/691. At the end of that same year, Abū Fudayk routed the Baṣrans, led by the brother of the Ummayyad governor (Ṭab.II, p.829, p.861, 1.10). But in the year 73/692, he was defeated by a combined army of Baṣrans and Kūfans and was killed. His army was surrounded in Mushaqqar and forced to surrender. 6,000 men are supposed to have been put to the sword (Ṭab. p.825s.). This was the downfall of the state of the Najadāt in Yamāma and Baḥrayn.[21,22]

---

1. He kept the Khawārij in prison and thereby tried to ensure a claim on the gratitude of the Baṣrans. (Ṭab.II, p.433).

2. cf. The Kāmil, p.604, 1.18 - p.608, 1.12.

3. Ibn Azraq was in fact not a Tamīmite (Ḥanẓalite Ṭab.II, p.517) but a Bakrite of Ḥanīfa (The Kāmil, p.541, 1.16, p.604, 1.12. Anon. Ahlw.

p.78, 1.1). ʿAbīda b. Hilāl was also a Bakrite, but from Yashkūr.

4. Nāfiʿ b. Azraq was the son of a manumitted Greek blacksmith. (L)

5. In Ṭab.II, p.573, he is called Zuhayr erroneously. He was the son of ʿAlī b. Māhūz, whilst ʿAbdalla and ʿUbaydalla were sons of Bashīr b. Māhūz. See Anon. p.80 and The Kāmil p.609 for this family. Their head was supposed to have been, according to The Kāmil, p.609, Ḥassān b. Bahdaj, who is also mentioned in Anon. p.149, 1.4. But this man was a Bakrite (of Ḥanīfa), the brother of ʿAbd al-Raḥmān b. Baḥzaj, who first fought under Najdā and then roved around Fārs and constantly annoyed ʿUmar b.b. Maʿmar. (Anon. p.137, 1.16, pp.148ss.)

6. According to Anon. Ahlw., p.79, 1.15, that happened at the end of Shawwāl, 64 (middle of June, 684).

7. A more detailed account of these events is given in the EI. The Khārijites assassinated the sub-governor, Masʿūd b. ʿAmr and refused to recognise the governor sent by ʿAbdalla b. al-Zubayr, ʿUmar b. ʿUbaydalla. He took control of Kūfa with local help and expelled Nāfiʿ, who, reinforced, retook the town and drove out ʿUmar. Ibn al-Zubayr then sent another army headed by Muslim b. ʿUbays. At this point the Khārijites divided, with Nāfiʿ leaving Baṣra to continue the struggle. EI, I, p.810. (L)

8. The Asāwira were a regiment of Persian cavalry who surrendered to the Arabs at Tustar, converted to Islam and took up service with the Arab armies in Baṣra. (L)

9. Ṭab.II, p.433, 1.20, p.441, 1.1, p.442, 1.5, p.517, 1.20. In fact ʿUbaydalla would appear to have freed the prisoners on his arrival (The Kāmil, p.594) and not on his departure.

10. A good example of "death-mania" - of Istiʿrāḍ. (Istiʿrāḍ is more adequately defined on p.41.)

11. Shārī is simply another term for Khārij, meaning a schismatic. According to Lane's dictionary, the term is derived from the meaning one who sells: "We have sold ourselves in obedience to God", or "Verily God had purchased us and our possessions". Qā'id applied to one who holds back or is inactive. As applied to the Khārijites, a qā'id was one who "held back from aiding Alee and from fighting against him"; one of the Khārijites who did not go forth to war. (L).

12. These principles of Ibn Azraq are mentioned in connection with Najdā in the account of Anon. Ahlwardt. The meaning of Taqiya (not Baqiya) is made clear from Anon. p.142, l.4.

13. cf. Anon. p139, ll,5,6 and Ibn al-Athīr IV, p.168, l.18s.

14. He is supposed then to have been only 30 years old (Ibn al-Athīr, p.166, l.6) but his son Muṭarraḥ was already grown up (p.166, l.20). cf. Yāqūt II, p.450s.

15. Already previously he had undertaken an expedition there. (Anon. p.128).

16. The year 67. Thus correct in Ṭab.II, p.752, l.3 and Anon., p.133, l.8. The statement that it happened only in the year 69, when Muṣ'ab was Governor of Baṣra (Anon. p.133, l.5, Ibn al-Athīr p.166, l.23) does not suit the chronological sequence. The confusion is easily explained,and also the numbers seven and nine are difficult of distinguish in the Arabic script.

17. When that happened is unclear. cf. also Ibn Baḥzaj, p.51, note 5.

18. The year 68/687, Ṭab.II, p.782, l.1. Anon. p.137, l.6. Ibn al-Athīr p.168, l.2.

19. This must have been in the year 69/688. Henceforth there are no more dates until the death of Najdā, in the year 72/691. Of his officials in Yemen, Hārūq was prominent. In the verses of Anon. p.140, he is also named as Hurāq. cf. Ibn al-Athīr p.168, l.19.

20. It is noteworthy to see how far they were removed from a popular election in the Graeco-Roman, or modern sense.

21. cf. again Ibn al-Athīr, V, p.88s.

22. For a review of the doctrines of the Najdā and the Azāriqa see Watt, Khārijite Thought, pp.220-222. (L)

CHAPTER 9.

We now return to the year 65/684 and to the Azāriqa in Ahwāz who, although they took their name from a Ḥanafite, consisted essentially of Tamīmites in so far as they were Arabs at all. The account of Abū Mikhnaf has previously been taken to the point where Ibn Azraq advanced against Baṣra and Bābba, the Governor of Baṣra, sent the ʻAbdshamsite Muslim b. ʻUbays b. Kurayz to oppose him. Abū Mikhnaf goes on to say (Ṭab.II, pp.581ss.) that Muslim forced Ibn Azraq back to Dūlāb on the Dujail, that well known boundary river and scene of many battles. A bitter fight took place on the east bank of the river. Muslim was killed along with Ibn Azraq. Did the latter create such a profound impression in spite of, or perhaps because of, his speedy end? In addition, the following leaders were killed: Ḥajjāj b. Bāb al-Ḥimyarī on the Baṣran and ʻAbdalla b. Māḥūz on the Khārijite side. Now the Tamīmite Rabīʻa al-Ajdham assumed command of the former and ʻUbaydalla b. Māḥūz that of the latter. At the critical moment, reinforcements reached the Azāriqa and so they were victorious. Rabīʻa was killed, his troops fled across the river and many were drowned. But the Tamīmite Ḥāritha b. Badr, who had taken over the flag, covered the retreat and held his position on the other bank with a band of brave troops who stood by him. This account by Abū Mikhnaf should be compared with three parallel accounts in Anon. Ahlw., pp.85ss., in the Kitāb al-Aghānī vol.VI, pp.3ss. and in The Kāmil, pp.616ss., all of which should be taken together. The best version of the principal source, Madā'inī, is found in the Anonymous text. Although Madā'inī differs a little from Abū Mikhnaf in the names of the leaders and their order of succession, they are in agreement on essential points, but Madā'inī gives a more detailed account. According to him, the battle lasted for a month, until the twentieth day after the death of Ibn Azraq. The Baṣrans numbered originally 10,000 men but many deserted. The Azāriqa were 600 strong. The reinforcements who came from Yamāma numbered some 40 or 200 men. The battle took place in Jumādā II, 65, (Dec. - Jan. 684/5), sixteen months before the battle of Sillabra.[1] In The Kāmil and Aghānī, Madā'inī's account is filled out with anecdotal trimmings which, according to Brünnows's supposition, derive from Ibn Khidāsh.

Bābba had to give up the governorship after this defeat. He was replaced by ʿUmar b. ʿUbaydalla b. Maʿmar, also a Qurayshite, but an able man. Abū Mikhnaf ignores him completely and has Qubaʿ following immediately after Bābba (p.582, l.19) passing over something like half a year. As a result, he also omitted to mention a battle which was fought under ʿUmar against the Azāriqa. He is a much less reliable authority for Baṣran affairs than for those of Kūfa. According to Madā'inī (Anon. pp.97ss. The Kāmil, pp.623ss.), ʿUmar immediately sent a new army from Baṣra against them but, instead of Ḥāritha b. Badr who had held out with Tamīmites at Nahr Tira and prevented the Khawārij from crossing the Dujail, he gave command to his own brother, ʿUthmân. However, he suffered a bad defeat and was killed, whereupon Ḥāritha had to step in yet again to cover the retreat and to guard the former positions. The verses of a Tamīmite poet definitely prove that Madā'inī is correct (Anon. p.99); it is also understandable that a new army should have been sent from Baṣra against the Azāriqa in order to protect the capital. But because the two battles took place there in the same year (65/684) and were both fought on the east bank of the Dujail,[2] with Ḥāritha playing the same role on both occasions, it is not surprising that they are referred to as the same battle. Like Abū Mikhnaf, Wahb b. Jarīr (Anon. p.84, Tab. p.580s., cf. p.465s.) knew of only one battle on the Dujail against the Azāriqa in the year 65/684 but, in contrast, he knows only of that fought under ʿUmar and not under Bābba. He suggests as the principal captain of the Baṣrans either ʿUthmān or Muslim b. ʿUbays or Ḥāritha b. Badr, according to choice!

After this new defeat, there ensued another change of governor in Baṣra; according to Ṭabarī II, p.601, this happened in Ramaḍān 65/684 but, according to Anon. pp.99, it was not until the beginning of 66/685. Qubaʿ began his reign; he was a Qurayshite, and no more! Ḥāritha b. Badr, who, with the remainder of the defeated army had again taken up position at Nahr Tira, did not exist as far as he was concerned. His soldiers were allowed to desert him and to return unpunished to Baṣra. So this brave, noble Tamīmite[3] finally fell victim to the Azāriqa. He was drowned in the Dujail whilst fleeing from them, for the ship in which he wished to escape overturned when another fully armed soldier sprang in from the steep bank. His death cleared the road to Baṣra for the enemy.

Abū Mikhnaf knows nothing of this, as he mentions Ḥāritha still later amongst the survivors.[4] In his version, the terror at Dūlāb is followed immediately by the nomination of Muhallab as chief of military operations and his victory at Sillabra. He packs the intervening period of sixteen months awkwardly together. If one bases one's opinion on Madā'inī's version in Anon. and in The Kāmil and takes that together with the events as related in Ṭabarī II, pp.590s., then it places the following construction on the circumstances which led to Muhallab's nomination and which ended with the battle of Sillabra.

ʻUbaydalla b. Māḥūz, the Amīr of the Azāriqa, moved his headquarters to Nahr Tira where Ḥāritha b. Badr had previously kept guard. Three months after his death, his cavalry appeared in Furāt, that is on the bank of the Tigris which lies opposite the city of Baṣra. They renewed the pontoon bridges over the wider branch of the river and advanced to the island in the centre, only being separated from the town by the narrower branch. From there they were in fact soon driven out again but they remained on the other bank after the bridges had been destroyed once more.[5] In this miserable situation, under coercion from the Baṣrans, Muhallab was charged with directing military operations. The terms which he demanded were granted him. He drove the Azāriqa from the Tigris, did not pursue them immediately, but spent the next forty days collecting the taxes on the other bank of the Tigris, for he had laid claim to the revenues for several years of those provinces from which he was supposed to expel the enemy. As soon as he had the money, more troops flocked to him. Then he turned towards the East and forced the Azāriqa slowly back, not without suffering some severe blows himself. His brother Muʻārik fell into their hands and was crucified. A bloody encounter at Ṣulāf remained indecisive, still on this side of the Dujail.[6] However, after that the enemy found it advisable to retreat across the river.

Muhallab pursued them and at Sillabra (or Silla) east of the Dujail, he won a decisive victory in Shawwāl 66 (May 686). The course of events in Abū Mikhnaf, who takes up the account again here, is described differently from other authorities, despite occasional agreement in one conspicuous detail. But it is clear that things were finely balanced between them for a long time. A section of the government troops fled, stopping only when they reached Baṣra. Muhallab himself, with his tribal supporters the Azd ʿUmān, saved the honour of the day. They vied with their rivals the Tamīmites, who until then had taken the honours in the battle with the Azāriqa. The latter were badly hit; people who previously had camped around five or six fires, now found room enough round only one. ʿUbaydalla b. Māḥūz himself was amongst those slain. A great many non-Arab people had joined them, indigenous folk who perhaps originally only wished to be rid of the tyrants and oppressors but who afterwards became the most fanatical of the fanatics and grew like a Hydra (The Kāmil, p.680). But the Azāriqa were no lowly rabble, as they were called by their enemies; on the contrary, as everyone accepts, they were the better armed and provided for. They had a particular superiority in cavalry. Naturally, the cavalry was also the main concern of their opponents for, if they lost their horses as they once did through lack of food (Ṭab.II, p.828), then they might as well return home. Muhallab is said to have introduced iron stirrups because the wooden ones broke too easily and the rider had no point of support in order to deliver a strong cut and thrust (The Kāmil, p.675).

I base the further stages of the story on Abū Mikhnaf's account according to Ṭabarī, for it is simpler, and I add to it only very slight complementary details which are indicated as such. After the serious defeat which they had suffered, the Azāriqa vacated Ahwāz and withdrew towards the East into the mountains. They were now led by Zubayr b. Māḥūz, a cousin of his two predecessors, ʿAbdalla and ʿUbaydalla b. Māḥūz. They still carried on skirmishing with Muhallab, particularly along the borders of Fārs and Ahwāz.[7] However, when Muṣ'ab became Governor of Baṣra at the end of 66/685 or the beginning of 67/686, and began the struggle against Mukhtār,[8] he persuaded Muhallab to play a leading role in his campaign. After Mukhtār had been killed (14 Ramaḍān = 3 April 687) he did not send him back to Fārs,[9] but sent him to Mosul to defend the borders of Iraq against the Syrians. At the same time he deposed his son Mughīra, who until then had represented Muhallab in Fārs (Anon. p.111, The Kāmil p.643), and replaced him by 'Umar b. 'Ubaydalla b. Ma'mar, probably still in the year 67/686 or at the beginning of 68/687. This man defeated the Azāriqa led by Zubayr at Sabūr (or Iṣṭakhr). They then retreated to the territory of Isfahān and Kirmān[10] but suddenly broke out again after a while and went through Fārs and Ahwāz in the direction of Baṣra. 'Umar pursued them, terrified because he had let them through. From Baṣra, Muṣ'ab himself turned to face them. Thereupon they withdrew to Kūfan territory in the direction of Madā'in and the Amīr of Madā'in fled. In this area they dealt barbarously with the Muslims, not sparing women and children. Abū Bakr b. Mikhnaf, who had a post there, was killed in the fight against them.[11]

Quba' was Governor in Kūfa, since Muṣ'ab had returned to Baṣra. He was in no hurry to oppose the Azāriqa. Ibn Ashtar offered to attack them himself but the other tribal leaders were mostly jealous of him. When Quba' finally got rid of the demons (i.e. the Khawārij!), they withdrew without a battle to Baṣran territory, where he left them in peace. They then crossed the Median mountains, fell upon Rayy[12] and besieged Isfahān. But the Kūfan Tamīmite 'Attāb b. Warqa defended the city tenaciously for several months. After a bold attack he finally occupied their camp and forced them to withdraw. Their Amīr Zubayr b. Māḥūz had been killed and, as his successor, they appointed another Tamīmite, the bold and intelligent Qaṭarī b. Fujā'a, who had a reputation as a poet.[13] This man led them back to Kirmān where they recuperated and replenished their strength. After doing that, they emerged and broke through Isfahān into Ahwāz and drove over the Dujail towards Ṣulāf. The Baṣrans were terror-stricken: their city was in grave danger for Muṣ'ab, as usual, was in the field against the Syrians. They wrote to him, saying that Muhallab had to come.[14] Muṣ'ab actually sent him back, after replacing him by Ibn Ashtar. Muhallab now raised an army in Baṣra, marched against the Azāriqa and skirmished with them for eight months at Ṣulāf, until the battle of Maskin when Muṣʻab was defeated by ʻAbd al-Malik and killed. The news of this decisive catastrophe reached the Khawārij before Muhallab. They took advantage of it in order to bring to light the lack of political consciousness of the Baṣrans. They asked them "What is your opinion of Muṣʻab?" "He is our Imām, who keeps to the right way, our leader in this world and the next and we are his followers in Life and in Death." "And what is your opinion of ʻAbd al-Malik?" "We curse him and want nothing to do with him in this world and the next, we are his enemies in Life and in Death and would shed his blood more joyfully than yours." "But Muṣʻab has been killed by ʻAbd al-Malik and tomorrow you will recognise as your Imām the victor, whom today you curse and shun."[15] The Azāriqa had formed a correct impression of their enemies. When the news of Muṣʻab's defeat was confirmed, Muhallab made his troops pay homage to ʻAbd al-Malik (Ṭab.II, pp.753ss., p.821s.).

These events occupy a long period of time, from the end of 66 (Summer 686) until the beginning of 72/691, for Muṣʻab was killed in Jumādā 72 (Autumn 691). Abū Mikhnaf gives only a very few dates. After the death of Mukhtār on 14 Ramaḍān 67 (3 April 687), Muṣʻab stayed a whole year in Kūfa, whilst someone else acted as governor for a while in Baṣra, (his nephew Ḥamza b. ʻAbdalla b. Zubayr, Ṭab.II, p.752, ll.13-14). Then he returned to Baṣra approximately around Ramaḍān 68. Therefore, the invasion of Kūfan territory by the Azāriqa can only be placed towards the end of 68/687 and they would not have reached Isfahān before 69/688. They stayed a long time in that area besieging the capital for several months (seven according to The Kāmil, p.649). Therefore Qaṭarī did not become Caliph before the end of 69/688, or perhaps even later. One can assume that he rested the following year in Kirmān, in order to re-organise his troops, and then emerged again ready for battle in Ahwāz around the beginning of 71/690. Muhallab's preparations and his eight-month long skirmishing at Ṣulāf would then occupy the year 71/690 and the beginning of the following year. Ṭabarī, thoughtless as ever, packs wherever possible all these events into the year 68/687 and jumps from the end of that year to the year 72/691. The sections for the years 69/688 and 70/689 remain altogether empty in his account. Not only these points but in general terms, experience demonstrates the difficulties of the chronology of that period marked by the battles between ʻAbd al-Malik and Muṣʻab.

The parallel account in Anon. and The Kāmil contains, as usual, more detail than that of Abū Mikhnaf. It differs on three points in particular: I) When Zubayr b. Māḥūz threatened Baṣra and then turned aside to Madā'in, Ḥamza b.b. Zubayr, who was then in fact Governor of Baṣra, was the next to oppose him. Then it was Muṣ'ab who opposed him again, after he had returned from Kūfa to his old post. To await the change of Governor, Zubayr would have had to remain for a remarkably long time in a very dangerous position, threatened in the rear by ʻUmar b.b. Maʻmar. II) Muhallab had already been sent back from Mosul to Baṣra when Zubayr burst out from Kirmān to Ahwāz and not just at a later stage when Qaṭarī emerged in similar fashion. He certainly did not go into action before the year 71/690. Besides, his successor in Mosul, Ibn Ashtar, was still in Kūfa at the end of 68/687. III) The battle-field in the year 71/690 was not near Ṣulāf but on the other side of the Dujail in various places in the region of Ramhurmuz. Here Abū Mikhnaf seems to have made a mistake, doing so all the more easily because he knows nothing of the battles of Muhallab at Ṣulāf in the year 66/685.

The transition of Iraq to the rule of ʻAbd al-Malik did not improve the situation in so far as it was determined by the Khawārij. He entrusted the governorship to the Umayyads who forced Muhallab into the background to gain prominence for themselves. Khālid, the great-grandson of Asīd came to Baṣra. He personally assumed command against the Azāriqa, with the result that he led his army into a very dangerous situation at Nahr Tira and was quite happy to escape as a result of Muhallab's vigilance. After that, the Khawārij returned to Kirmān and Khālid himself returned to Baṣra, giving command of the army and the pursuit of the campaign to his brother ʻAbd al-ʻAzīz whom he brought back to Fārs in place of ʻUmar b.b. Maʻmar. ʻAbd al-ʻAzīz suffered a serious defeat near Darābjird; he himself escaped but he lost the greater part of his army and left his beautiful wife prisoner in the hands of his enemies. Fortunatly for her, she was killed. At the same time, another brother of Khālid, Umayya, was slain in Baḥrayn by Abu Fūdayk, who worked with his Najadāt (more or less) in agreement with Qaṭarī.[16] The victorious Azāriqa pursued the fleeing Baṣrans back over the bridge of Arbuk, conquered the whole of Ahwāz and advanced up to Furāt Maysān opposite Baṣra. (The Kāmil, p.663, l.9). The situation in 73-4/692-3 was again exactly as it had been in the year 65/684 after the Battle of Dūlāb. Muhallab, with his handful of men, had not been able to halt the enemy and had followed those who had fled to Baṣra. Now he was able to gloat over the trouble caused by these inquisitive haughty princes of Umayya. He knew that now the time was ripe for him.

Such is the account in The Kāmil, pp.654ss. Abū Mikhnaf, according to Ṭabarī, II, pp.821ss., tells the story in opposite order; first comes the unlucky campaign of ʿAbd al-ʿAzīz, then the more fortunate one of Khālid which also had an unhappy sequel, although not such a bad effect, namely that the Azāriqa reached the bank of the Tigris lying opposite Baṣra by coming through Ahwāz. This latter fact is confirmed by the contemporary verses of Kaʿab al-Ashqarī, according to Ṭabarī, II, pp.1010s.: the Baṣrans were in the greatest danger; they did not dare cross the bridge until eventually Muhallab was given command and forced the Azāriqa back to Ramhurmuz. Here it is proved at the same time that, in this case, the account of The Kāmil takes precedence over that of Abū Mikhnaf.

Henceforth, Abū Mikhnaf's account (Ṭab.II, pp.855ss., pp.873ss., pp.1,003ss.) and that of The Kāmil (pp.661ss.) coincide, so that one can compare them synoptically and complete one from the other. ʿAbd al-Malik deposed Khālid b. Asīd and gave his brother, Bishr b. Marwān, control over Baṣra in addition to Kūfa. But above all he entrusted Muhallab with command against the Azāriqa and in such a way that he was autonomous of the Governor, giving him the right to recruit troops in Baṣra. In addition, Bishr had to put a Kūfan army at his disposition but he instructed its commander, the Azdite ʿAbd al-Raḥmān b. Mikhnaf,[17] to disobey Muhallab's orders and to thwart his aims, for he had a grudge against Muhallab as he was nominated directly by the Caliph and not subordinate to him.

Fortunately, Ibn Mikhnaf knew better where his duty lay. The Azāriqa were now driven back over the Dujail into the mountains. The Baṣrans and Kūfans established a strong camp at Ramhurmuz. After they had been there for ten days, news came that Bishr had died in Baṣra. As a result, most of the Kūfans and also many Baṣrans left the camp and went home. They refused to be restrained by their leaders, who now had only a few men left with them. The effect of this political event throws some light on the military discipline of the Iraqi soldiers. It is remarkable that their enemies do not seem to have taken advantage of the situation. (One must assume that) Muhallab was still strong enough to defend himself behind walls and trenches and that the Azd, who made up his tribe and that of his army, would have held out with him.

Subsequently, the death of Bishr proved a great gain for Muhallab for al-Ḥajjāj replaced Bishr at the beginning of the year 75/694 and gave Muhallab the trusty support which he needed. The first thing which the new Governor did was to drive those who had fled, out of Kūfa and Baṣra back to Ramhurmuz. He himself came to the camp and, on this occasion, subdued with bloody severity a mutiny of the ʿAbd al-Qays of Baṣra, at the beginning of Shaʿbān 75. At the end of Shaʿbān 75 (December 694) Muhallab was able to go over to the attack. The Azāriqa withdrew back to Fārs and he followed them via Arjān and Saradān to Kāzarūn in the territory of Sabūr. There he and the Baṣrans established a strong fortified camp, as he always used to do. The Kūfans were less cautious and had to pay the price. During a night attack by the Azāriqa, which Muhallab fortunately repelled, the majority of the Kūfans were destroyed; seventy of their most distinguished and oldest Qur'ān Readers were killed, in addition to their leader Ibn Mikhnaf (Tuesday-Wednesday 20 Ramaḍān 75 = 12 Jan. 695). As a replacement al-Ḥajjāj ordered ʿAttāb b. Warqa with the Kūfan garrison from Isfahān to go to Kāzarūn (76/695). But after eight months at the beginning of 77/696, he called him back again because he was needed more in Iraq (against Shabīb) and also because he had started a dangerous quarrel with Muhallab which threatened to break out as a tribal feud between the Tamīm and the Azd in the army. After the fighting in the region of Sabūr and Iṣṭakhr had gone on for more than a year, the

Azāriqa finally evacuated Fārs and went back to the province of Kirmān, which for a long time had been completely in their power. First they went to Sīrajān; driven out from there they established themselves in the town of Jīraft. Muhallab pursued them there also. After they left Fārs, he still had to fight with them for about eighteen months before he overcame them. al-Ḥajjāj suspected him of deliberately prolonging the war in order to hold on to his command and its benefits. He kept him under close scrutiny and, as soon as Fārs was pacified, he withdrew the province from his command along with its taxes, except for a small amount needed for the upkeep of the troops. Again and again he sent legates to him to urge him to hurry. However, he could not make Muhallab change his mind: in this situation, the latter preferred not to rush violently ahead but to wait. He was hoping for sickness, hunger, or inner strife amongst the enemy.[18] The inner strife indeed arose: the Azāriqa treated Qaṭarī just as the Najadāt had treated Najdā. They scrutinized him carefully and reproached him for his transgressions. They were rebellious when he stood his ground, protected his officials, did not reply to their questions about the principle of assassination as they would have wished and generally would not do immediately what they wanted. Also a more general conflict was at the root of it all: the Arabs in the army as a rule supported Qaṭarī; the Mawālī opposed him and promoted one of their own number, ʿAbd Rabbihi the younger. They were in the majority, altogether 8,000 men, and all deeply versed in the Qur'ān. Some Arabs, led by ʿAmr al-Qanā had joined them. Bloody skirmishes arose between the two parties, lasting for about a month. Muhallab looked on calmly because he feared that his intervention would be the best means of uniting the hostile brethren. The Arabs, led by Qaṭarī and ʿAbdīda b. Hilāl, lost, were driven out of the city and, after a while, marched away to Ṭabaristān. Now Muhallab only had to deal with the Mawālī led by ʿAbd Rabbihi. They were finally defeated by him and were totally destroyed. Thus he had fulfilled his task and he returned to Baṣra where he was received with due honour and rewarded with the Governorship of Khurāsān. (78/697).

The war waged by Muhallab against the Azāriqa was fought under the overall command of al-Ḥajjāj and began after the middle of 75/694. It lasted according to Ka'ab al-Ashqarī (Ṭab. II, p.1,014, l.1) all in all for three years, that is until the middle of 78/697. The chronology of Abū Mikhnaf is confused because Ṭabarī II, p.1,003 says that after the recall of 'Attāb which took place at the beginning of 77/696,[19] Muhallab had fought for about a year in Fārs and another year and a half in Kirmān: with that one would reach the end of 79/698. The words "after the recall of 'Attāb" are erroneous; correctly they should read "after the arrival of 'Attāb in Kāzarūn". They probably derive not from Abū Mikhnaf but from Ṭabarī, who, after a lengthy interruption, picks up again the threads which he had let fall on II, p.878. This addition is also lacking in the otherwise identical passage, Ṭab.II, p.880. It can be concluded from the details in The Kāmil (p.676, l.18, p.677, ll.15s.) that 'Attāb was only called home after the end of the campaign in Fārs, this being also the most appropriate conclusion. Then everything fits somehow together. The war in Ahwāz began after the middle of 75/694. The battles in Fārs lasted longer than a year, until the beginning of 77/696, and those in Kirmān ended towards the middle of 78/697, taking about another year and a half.

Only Abū Mikhnaf's account in Ṭabarī,II, pp.1,018ss. gives a coherent version of the Arabian Azāriqa who had gone from Kirmān to Ṭabaristān led by Qaṭarī and 'Abīda b. Hilāl. Sufyān b. al-Abrad al-Kalbī was sent against them with the Syrians, after he had finished off Shabīb at the end of 77/696 on the Dujail. He was assisted by the Kūfan garrison at Ṭabaristān, led by Isḥāq b. Ash'ath, and the garrison at Rayy, led by Ja'far b. 'Abd al-Raḥmān b. Mikhnaf. Qaṭarī was trapped in a ravine in Ṭabaristān, his companions were scattered and he himself fell from his horse into a deep abyss. One of the inhabitants of that area saw him lying there, shattered his hips with a stone, and then told a group of Kūfans who killed him. Abū 'l-Jahm who had to avenge his father, cut off his head and was sent with it to the Caliph who rewarded him by giving pensions to his children. Thereupon, Sufyān turned his attentions to 'Abīda b. Hilāl and besieged him in a castle at Qumis, where he and his followers had established themselves. He refused the challenge to give himself up. His resigned but determined swan-song is preserved for us. The besieged ones were starved out and were all slain in a final sortie. They suffered this fate about the same time as their former companions in Jīraft in the year 78/697. Thus the Azāriqa were eradicated from the face of the earth. They did not continue to exist as a sect because they were too much men of action, but tradition and poetry provide a firm memorial to the fact that they had held the Islamic East in check for many years. It is not correct, as happens in more recent publications, to dismiss them with a few phrases. They were overcome at least as much by their own disintegration as by the strategy of Muhallab, who made his name by conquering them. The Arabs and the Mawālī did not get on together; Nature proved stronger than Principle!

---

1. See p.58.

2. But the name Dūlāb is only applied to the first battle. Dāris is given as the site of the second one in The Kāmil p.671, l.9.

3. About him cf. Agh. vol.XXI, pp.20ss.

4. Ṭab.II, p.585. The verse on p.580, l.17, p.585, l.6 and Anon. p.100, l.12 is situated in an inconsistent, arbitrary context.

5. Furāt is not the Euphrates (Brünnow p.72) but the territory on the left bank of the Tigris opposite Baṣra, belonging to Maysān. In the middle of the river lay an island to which went the pontoon bridges. The large branch of the river is called the large bridge and the smaller branch, the small bridge, even when the bridge is temporarily destroyed. cf. Ṭab.II, p.590s. The Kāmil, pp.626ss.

6. The leader of the Tamīm was now Harīsh b. Hilāl, cf. the Index of The Kāmil and of Anon. Previously, we find him in Khurāsān (Madā'inī, according to Ṭab.II, pp.595ss.).

7. Anon. p.110. The Kāmil p.641. On one such occasion the sun underwent an eclipse (The Kāmil p.641, l.8); it must have taken place in the summer of 686.

8. See Section II, chapter 4.

9. False, according to Ibn al-Athīr IV, p.232.

10. It seems that Kirmān was completely in their power; they emerged from there and retreated there again.

11. Perhaps a relative of Abū Mikhnaf, for, according to the verses of the Azdite Surāqa (Ṭab.II, pp.757s.) he was a Sayyid of the Azd, and Abū Mikhnaf himself belonged to the Sayyid Family of the Azd of Kūfa.

12. Whether they undertook the expedition to Rayy (which is not mentioned in Abū Mikhnaf's account) before the siege of Isfahān or during it is not clear from Anon. p.118 and The Kāmil pp.647ss. According to Ibn al-Athīr, IV, p.236, it appears that they were invited by the inhabitants, or at least encouraged by them against the Government.

13. The chief poet of the Khawārij was ʿImrān b. Ḥiṭṭān, a pious man, well read in the Qurʾān and Tradition. (Agh. vol.XVI, pp.152ss.) They were thus in no way professed enemies of poetry, despite their piety, and they practised it in the traditional, essentially heathen style.

14. Ṭabarī, II, p.764, l.18 says that Qubaʿ was Muṣʾab's governor in Baṣra, the same man who had otherwise represented him in Kūfa. It is doubtful whether this is correct.

15. Although this story is perhaps too good to be true, yet it is not impossible. If arms were laid down for a time, the parties would settle their dispute with words, as is clear from Agh. vol.VI, p.6, vol.VII, p.59. It is also related there that during a fierce quarrel in Muhallab's camp about whether Jarīr or Farazdaq was the better poet, an appeal for settlement was made to a Khārijite - ʿAbīda b. Hilāl - and that he decided in favour of Jarīr.

16. See pp.59s.

17. A relative of the Traditionist Abū Mikhnaf.

18. Muhallab was in truth not so inactive as it appears according to this. In the verses of Ka'ab al-Ashqarī (Ṭab.II, pp.1,011-14) quite a few more or less famous battles are quoted, which are not found either in The Kāmil or in Abū Mikhnaf. His principal objective was indeed that the enemy should not break through at any point and suddenly appear in Baṣra.

19. The Kāmil p.677, l.15. Ṭab.II, p.944.

CHAPTER 10.

At the same time as Baṣra was endangered by the Azāriqa, Kūfa was threatened by other Khawārij who emerged from the region of Mosul. Abū Mikhnaf, according to Ṭabarī, II, pp.881-989, can be considered as the almost exclusive authority on them, in an account related with much detail. He is the most reliable authority for everything which concerns Kūfa.

The pious Ṣāliḥ b. Musarriḥ lived in Dārā, between Nisibis and Mārdīn. For a long time he was the leader in that area of the Khawārij, who were in league with Kūfa, and from there they spread their creed. (Ṭab.II, p.881, p.977). He himself was a Tamīmite but that area on both sides of the Tigris consisted mainly of Arabs of Rabī'a, particularly the Banū Shaybān of Bakr, who not long previously had emigrated from their former residence on the right bank of the Euphrates in the Kūfan desert.[1] His followers lived amongst these people, he read the Qur'ān with them, taught them the Holy Law and preached sermons in which he urged them to be zealous for God, to avenge the sins of the rulers against men, and to fight against the false Imāms and their God-forsaken band.[2]

But he was in no hurry to act and is supposed to have taught and gathered support peacefully for twenty years. Only when forced, he finally led out his small band of troops.[3] On Wednesday, 1st. Ṣafar 76 (Friday, 21 May, 695) 100 to110 men joined him. Their first act was to plunder the Government stables in Dārā to obtain horses, for without them with their small numbers they could accomplish nothing. The inhabitants of Dārā, Nisibis and Sinjara fled before them into the citadels. Then in the market-place of Dhawjān during the public prayer they attacked and drove away 1,000 Qaysites sent against them by the governor Muḥammad b. Marwān.[4] Faced by a second Qaysite army, they left Muḥammad's province after a battle at Amid on the left bank of the Tigris and crossed into Kūfan territory.

Now al-Ḥajjāj came to deal with them sending three thousand Kūfans against them. The battle took place at the villages of Mudabbaj on the border of the provinces, on Tuesday 17 Jumādā I, 76 (Thursday, 3 September, 695). Things went badly for the Khawārij. Their leader Ṣāliḥ b. Musarriḥ was killed. They esteemed him highly and mourned him deeply but his death was no great loss for them, for it was only now that the right man emerged at their head: he was Shabīb b. Yazīd b. Nuʿaym from the distinguished family of Murra b. Ḥammām of Dhuhl b. Shaybān. Immediately he assumed command of the seventy or ninety remaining men and, with them, got through to the border territory belonging to Mosul, where he was safe from the Kūfans.[5] There also he was not inactive; he took revenge on certain of the tribal members of Shaybān and Anaza who were hostile to the Khawārij. Then, after he had taken his mother who lived in that region, he appeared again with 160 men in the territory of Madā'in which belonged to Kūfa, between the Tigris and the mountains, in particular the area of Jūkhā[6] around Nahrawān: this was the classic country of the Khawārij, sanctified through the bones of their oldest martyrs. In that area there were many Christian monasteries suitable as quarters and halting places for the soldiers. However, Shabīb retained no fixed position from which he marched out and into which he could withdraw. He always changed his residence. He immediately found opportunities of avenging the defeat of Mudabbaj as he defeated one government army after another at Khaniqīn and at Nahrawān. In this way he struck terror into the hearts of the Kūfans stationed at Madā'in and, consequently, they all stole away together to their homes.

al-Ḥajjāj now sent an army four thousand strong from Kūfa to Madā'in under the command of the Kindite Jazl. This man copied Muhallab's methods: he took the greatest care when pursuing the enemy into the territory of Jūkhā but did not leave them free there, pursuing them backwards and forwards and always fortifying himself at night. So he went on for two months until al-Ḥajjāj lost patience and replaced him with the Hamdānite Saʿīd b. Mujālid, ordering him to attack immediately. Shabīb was in Qaṭīṭiyā,[7] on the way to Barazruz, and had just ordered food for himself and his men when the local notable came to him trembling with the information that he was surrounded on all sides. Calmly he finished the meal, then got on his horse and broke through. When Sa'īd rode after him at the head of his cavalry, he turned round and struck him from his horse. The pursuers were terrified and fled, carrying with them the infantry remaining under Jazl's orders. Jazl himself was gravely wounded on this occasion, and al-Ḥajjāj sent him his personal physician to Madā'in.[8]

Shabīb now ventured even further. He went from Baghdād straight across country to Kūfa, shook off an army that was supposed to stand in his way and then crossed the Euphrates to Shaffān and Laṣāf in the desert, where he vented his rage on settled Bedouin relatives there because they declared his action was ruinous for the tribe. Then he disappeared into the far distance. al-Ḥajjāj thought that the air was now clear and went towards Baṣra. Then he got information that Shabīb was again approaching. Quickly he turned round; on the evening of the same day on which al-Ḥajjāj had returned, Shabīb appeared before Kūfa with 200 cavalry. During the night he sent his visiting card. He rode to the market place and rapped with a powerful blow of his club on the door of the citadel: the mark remained visible for a long time.[9] Next morning he was no longer there. Zayda b. Qudāma was sent after him with a considerable army but he could not find him where he searched. Shabīb had gone round in an arc and suddenly appeared again in Qādisiya on the other side of Kūfa. A troop of cavalry quickly thrown against him could not halt him; the capital stood open. But he preferred to fall upon Zayda b. Qudāma who was encamped twenty-four parasangs distant at Rudhbār. The surprise succeeded, Zayda was killed and his army was partly routed. But still Shabīb held back from pushing into Kūfa itself, although his men urged him to that. He preferred to go via Niffar, Ṣarāt and Baghdād back towards Khanijar on the other side of the Tigris.

al-Ḥajjāj suffered material damage as well as the blow to his pride: a large section of territory had been removed from his administration, that is to say his tax-control, and his treasure-houses had been plundered. Once again he sent a strong Kūfan army to Jūkhā, giving command to the well-known

'Abd al-Raḥmān b. Ash'ath al-Kindī. This man was guided by his predecessor and tribal companion Jazl and directed his military strategy according to Jazl's advice. Slowly he forced Shabīb back from the territory of Madā'in and, on express authorization, followed him over the border river Khawlāya into the areas of Daqūqa and Shahrazur, which were no longer subordinate to al-Ḥajjāj. Shabīb sought to exhaust him by zig-zag marches in the impassable mountain regions but had no opportunity to attack him. al-Ḥajjāj became impatient again and replaced the thoughtful Ibn Ash'ath by the impetuous 'Uthmān b. Qatan al-Ḥārithī.[10] This man took the bull by the horns but things went badly for him. On Thursday, 10 Dhū'l-Ḥijja 76 (Tuesday, 20 March, 696) he was defeated and killed at the town of Batta in the neighbourhood of the Khawlāya. Ibn Ash'ath led the retreat back to Dayr Abī Maryam and further to Kūfa.

Shabīb's achievement had been considerable in the winter season of 76 (695-6). In order to obtain the necessary rest for himself and his men, he took up summer residence at the beginning of 77 (April 696) in the mountains of Māh Bahrādhān.[11] During the three months that he remained there, his following increased. Many men joined him because they were pursued either by money- or by blood-debts. When the hot weather grew less intense - probably not yet in July or August - he went back to Madā'in. There a son of Mughīra, Mutarrif, reigned on behalf of al-Ḥajjāj but he bore little resemblance to his father. He had strong Khārijite tendencies and, although he was not exactly willing to subordinate himself to Shabīb, nor did he wish to oppose him in a hostile manner. Instead, he vacated the city and withdrew into the Median mountains where he met his death. With Madā'in, Shabīb gained a very important position but does not seem to have taken much advantage of it.

During the period in which his opponent had left him in peace, al-Ḥajjāj had taken the opportunity to raise an army, almost ten times larger than before. All the soldiers who were inscribed on the Dīwān of Kūfa had to join, young and old, among whom were such men as had already fought sixty years ago at Qādisiya. In addition, those troops who had been detached from Kūfa were conscripted, particularly those who helped the Baṣrans against the Azāriqa. Their leader ʿAttāb b. Warqa assumed the overall command. After Madāʾin had fallen into the hands of the Khawārij, that is after the hot season of the year 77/696, these crowds got on the move. They came as far as Sūq Ḥakama near Ṣarāt,[12] to the south-west of the Tigris not far from Baghdād. There Shabīb fell upon them with 600 men. It was an easy task for him; they were more like a herd than an army and the least of their faults was that they no longer knew the old war-songs and had no orator to stir them to enthusiasm. They left the battle to their leaders and champions and, after they had been killed, amongst them ʿAttāb b. Warqa himself, they all rushed away.

Thereafter Shabīb could go not only to terrify Kūfa but to attack it in earnest. After he had dispersed a small army on the way, he crossed the Euphrates unimpeded and pitched camp on the Sabakha in front of Kūfa. There he built a mosque, from which it would appear that his stay was not limited to a short period.[13] If al-Ḥajjāj had relied only on the Kūfans, it would have gone ill with him. Also his servants and Mawālī whom he armed, would probably not have saved him, although they were braver and more reliable. But he had at all events requested Syrian soldiers from the Caliph and these had arrived just in time, 4,000 men under the Kalbite Sufyān b. Abrad. The Syrians marched out to the Sabakha against the Khawārij and fought with them under the eyes of al-Ḥajjāj, who looked on from a high position sitting on his chair. Step by step they forced them back. The decisive moment came with an attack by the son of the fallen ʿAttāb and some Kūfans,[14] against Shabīb's camp: in the course of this his wife Ghazāla was slain. The Khawārij, who until then had fought hand to hand, jumped on their horses and fled across the Euphrates bridges. Shabīb was the last to leave the battlefield; slowly he rode back and deep in thought he shook his head. When his attention was drawn to the Syrians who were hard on his heels he turned around in an unconcerned way and turned in upon himself again, shaking his head. But al-Ḥajjāj called the pursuers back: "Leave them to God to burn in Hell-fire!" The battle took place barely before the middle of the year 77/696. A more exact date is not given.

Shabīb came through another battle in Anbār,

then with the remainder of his cavalry - for many had deserted him - he withdrew to Jūkhā. But even there he was not able to stay for long: he decided to go to Kirmān, where the Azāriqa were still undefeated. He was already on that side of the Dujayl, in Ahwāz, when the Syrians led by Sufyān b. Abrad came after him, but he crossed the river again to meet them.[15] The Syrians withstood his furious attack and he found it advisable to cross to the other bank during the following night. But as he passed over the bridges last of all behind his men, his stallion reared up, tripped and plunged into the water. Shabīb in his heavy armour was helpless. He drowned with the following words: "Thus is the will of the Almighty, the Omniscient!" This was probably still in 77/696, towards the end of the year. The powerfully built corpse of the hero excited the astonishment of the Syrians. His mother was still alive; she was a woman of Greek origin taken prisoner in battle. Until that time she always disbelieved the reports of the death of her son which reached her now and then, but when she heard that he was drowned, she believed it. For, according to a dream which she had had before his birth, her fire-brand could only be extinguished in water.[16] The death of Shabīb in the waters of the Dujayl seemed to correspond with this; it also remained firmly fixed in the memory of posterity.[17]

There are signs which indicate in addition that Shabīb was killed not merely because of the superiority of his enemies, but also perhaps through the quarrelsome nature and jealousy of his friends. According to ʿUmar b. Shabba in Ṭabarī II, p.967, precisely at the critical moment in the battle, the Ḍabbite Maṣqala b. Muhalhil caught hold of his reins and asked him: "What say you of Ṣāliḥ b. Musarriḥ, and what is your opinion of him?" Shabīb was astonished at being asked to pronounce on that in such circumstances, but he refused to modify his standpoint and thereby caused the defection of Maṣqala and his numerous companions as they withdrew to one side. In this manner, victory was made easy for al-Ḥajjāj.

According to a variant reading which Abū Mikhnaf himself adds to his main account (Ṭab.II, pp.975s.), treachery was afoot in the catastrophe of the Dujayl: Shabīb did not come safely over the bridges because his own companions had cut the ropes.[18]

In fact that sounds more probable than the reported legendary feature of his stallion rearing up because there was a mare in front of him. Amongst the small bands which he led there were many who were in no sense attached to him body and soul. This was hardly appropriate for people who recognized only God as their banner. They reproached him for making exceptions of his relatives from the prescribed bloody severity against unbelievers and so they were particularly zealous in killing these people. They blamed him for adopting the "Taqiya" doctrine, saying that he let prisoners go free if they pronounced the K͟hārijite formula "Only God has the power of Decision", and that he put this directly into their mouths in order to save them (Ṭab.II, pp.967s.). It made no difference to them that his mildness was at the same time a form of prudence and that this was the reason why many Kūfans did not defend themselves until the last drop of blood. But above all, his personal superiority aroused the hatred of envious people, such as that Ḍabbite Maṣqala, who tried to defeat living authority by causing the death of the founder of the party.

He towered above his companions in stature and in physical strength and also in courage. However, he was not merely a dare-devil. The reports of the various bold strokes with which he, like Samson, scorned and terrified the Philistines and their task-master, only show one side of him. He was also prudent and cautious. He had only a very small army at his disposition, the hard core of which depended upon his Shaybānite tribal companions: there is no talk of Mawālī. He had to make do with his few cavalry. Therefore he took care that they should be well-armed and supplied, and also well-rested. He found enough money in the treasure houses of the Government. He made good the disadvantage of lesser numbers through his astonishing mobility in suitable, well-chosen, terrain. He avoided the enemy when they wished to catch him and fell upon them when they least expected it. He was usually informed of their movements because he was on the best of terms with the Christian inhabitants of the territory. They saw in him an accomplice against their oppressor and, although they did not dare to take his part openly, yet they proved of useful service to him where they could.[19] He was also particularly well-versed in exploiting the resources of the small campaign. Yet, in spite of all, he was not completely absorbed in his affairs. He was a man of ingenuity and unusual qualities which he did not merely demonstrate with words. How distressed people would be when he allowed the gorgeous money which fell into his hands from the treasure houses of Samarraja, roll back from the rear of the mule into the canal! He was capable of showing a careless indifference in the greatest danger. After his first defeat, he was far away in his thoughts from what was going on around him. Was he thinking of the loss of his wife, from whom he was inwardly and outwardly inseparable? More likely, than of the loss of the battle, for he did not sell his soul entirely to the affairs which he directed. He was too human for that. Without doubt the fanatics of the party were aware of this. That which gained him the sympathy of others (also of Abū Mikhnaf), aroused their hatred. It is tragic that he had to squander his talent in the service of such people. In these circumstances, his exit is not without some compensation. The glowing meteor was scattered over high Heaven.[20]

---

1. The mother of the Shaybānite Shabīb lived in the region of Mosul, on the slopes of Mount Satidama (Blood-drinker). Doubtless his deceased father had lived in the same place. But the family had emigrated there (via Kūfa, Ṭab. II, p.977) from the watering-place Laṣāf in the Kūfan desert (Ḥamāsa p.15). A section of the relatives remained there and ofter received visits from Shabīb's parents (Ṭab.II, p.915, p.978). Perhaps the break up of the Shaybānites was not totally of their own accord but was caused by Muʿāwiya.

2. There existed a written collection of these sermons, of which one example is passed on. (Ṭab.II, p.881s.)

3. The Shaybānite Faḍāla b. Sayyār had already defected from him and had been killed previously (Ṭab.II, p.893s.).

4. The Qays lived in Southern Mesopotamia. The Governor lived amongst them in Ḥarrān. (Ṭab.II, p.887, l.9, l.15, p.889, l.2, p.1,377, ll.3&5.)

5. It is called Jāl. (Ṭab.II, p.893, l.7, p.94, l.16, p.95, l.5.) Mount Satidama seems to have been there. cf. Hoffmann's Auszüge, note 1488.(Auszüge aus Syrischen Akten Persischer Märtyrer, G. Hoffmann, Leipzig 1880). Abū Mikhnaf's account of Shabīb contains much geographical material.

6. Anbār (Ṭab.II, p.980, l.11) and al-Ustān (p.929, l.12) also belonged to Madā'in.

7. Not far from Nahrawān (Ṭab.II, p.908, l.2, p.909, l.2). Nahrawān is properly speaking a canal (with many branches) and then, in addition, the name of a place.

8. Here there is a variant Ṭab.II, p.911, l.18 - p.915, l.1. With p.915, l.1, the thread let fall at p.911, l.18, is picked up again.

9. The story that Shabīb, by his intrusion into Kūfa, enabled his wife Ghazāla to fulfil her vow to pray in the mosque there, is missing from Abū Mikhnaf's account. (According to him, Shabīb entered the mosque in order to slay several people praying at night, whom he found still there.) The story occurs in Mas'ūdī, V, p.321 and Aghani, XVI, p.155 and appears to be referred to in a verse (Mas'ūdī, V, p.441) in which Ghazāla is called "the woman with the vow". However, cf. p.73, n.13. Noteworthy is Ṭab.II, p.767.

10. Son of Ḥusayn, Ṭab.II, p.982, l.3, namely the well-known Ḥusayn Dhū 'l-Ghuṣṣa. The Kūfan leaders are usually their most distinguished men.

11. Ṭab.II, p.941. The locality is not known to me. Ṭab.II, p.982 relates a different version, that Shabīb came from Satidama to Madā'in.

12. Ṣarāt, like Nahrawān, is both a canal and a place.

13. Or did he build it only so that Ghazāla could fulfil her vow? It stood for a long time and bore his name. Al-Ḥajjāj had the head of Shabīb's wife cut off and buried there; she was supposed to have been carried to him after

her death.

14. Ṭab.II, p.961, p.967. From that it is clear that the Kūfans also took part in the battle besides the Syrians, contradicting Ṭab.II, p.955. ʿUmar b. Shabba, whose account Ṭabarī quotes as a variant to that of Abū Mikhnaf (p.962, 1.5 - p.968, 1.17) speaks however only of the Kūfans. Perhaps he was silent about the Syrians on purpose.

15. According to Abū Mikhnaf he had already come to Kirmān and had rested there.

16. The dream is based on the (false) derivation of the name Shabīb from an homonymous root which means "to burn". According to Yaʿqūbī (II, p.328) his mother was called Jahīza.

17. Also Theophanes A.M. 6185 mentions something of this: Shabīb advanced into Khurāsān and almost caused al-Ḥajjāj to be drowned in the river. Almost!

18. According to Yaʿqūbī II, p.328, the Syrians had cut the ropes. But then they must have won the battle. However Yaʿqūbī cannot be considered on the same level as Abū Mikhnaf.

19. When he pitched camp opposite the Kūfans on the Khawlāya, in the Church of Batta, the Christian inhabitants came to him and said: "You have a heart inclined towards us who are oppressed, you lend your ear to everyone and consider his complaint. But these Kūfans are tyrants who accept no excuse and if they hear that you set up your quarters in our Church, they will slay us after you have gone. So we beg you, transfer your camp to some other place near to our city." He also did them this kindness.

20. The reference is to the meaning of the word Shabīb; see Lane's Lexicon, p.1494. (Ed.)

CHAPTER 11.

After the death of Shabīb, his group was of no further significance. But the Khawārij still existed in the region of Moṣul amongst the Shaybān and the remaining Bakrites and from time to time they rose to action. Their saint was in fact not Shabīb but his predecessor Ṣāliḥ b. Musarrih, from whose collected sermons they derived edification and whose grave they visited with shaven heads.[1] Ṣāliḥ is considered as one of the Ṣufrites (Ṭab.II, p.880, l.16) who were not so barbaric and cruel as the Azāriqa. However, they maintained this more orderly attitude only as long as they remained peacefully within the Community of Catholic Muslims and they immediately became more violent when they rose in revolt and took to their swords. The difference is of little significance. If the Ṣufrites who fought under Shabīb were as they are described, then they adopted in all essential points the general characteristics of the Khawārij. Later there were several Khārijite sects in that region on the Tigris, who on occasion attacked each other fiercely.[2] Some had white and others black banners or turbans. (Ṭab.II, p.1624, p.1898).

Almost all the Khārijite revolts of which we hear in the later Umayyad period started from Mosul amongst the Bakrites. Under Yazid II, Shawdhab began a rebellion (Bisṭām in Ṭab.II, p.1378, l.17) with cavalry from Shaybān and Yashkūr. (Ṭab.II, p.1378, l.12, l.15.) His main district was the territory of Jūkhā. He defeated the Kūfans and the Qays of Ḥarrān but, finally, was defeated by the Syrians. Under Hishām II, Bahlūl b. Bishr[3] moved out from Moṣul against the Iraqi governor Khālid al-Qaṣrī whose troops he defeated twice, but finally he was himself defeated in the battle of Kuhayl near Moṣul. About the same time, a son of the famous Shabīb, Ṣaḥārī, with 30 Bakrites of Jabbul,[4] made an attack upon one of Khālid's estates but he had no success, fled over the Dujayl and was massacred at Manādhir. The chronicler for these three events is Abū ʿUbayda, according to Ṭabarī, II, pp.1348s, pp.1375ss., pp.1622ss., pp.1633s.

The Khārijite movement took on a totally different character when the Umayyad kingdom began to break up altogether: it now became part of a revolution. The difference is outwardly visible in the numbers. The small numbers of troops which usually are characteristic of the Khārijite armies, swelled to powerful masses. After the murder of Walīd II, the Shaybānite Saʿīd b. Bahdal arose in Mesopotamia, first got rid of a rival who also belonged to the Rabīʿa and then turned against Kūfa. But on the way, he died of the plague; his successor was Ḍaḥḥāk b. Qays al-Shaybānī (Ṭab.II, p.1900, l.4). This man had several thousand troops under his banner; the Ṣufrites of Shahrazur[5] joined him, but performed the prayers under their own Imām. Also there were many women in the army who fought bravely in men's armour.[6] In Kūfa and Ḥīra the former governor, a son of ʿUmar II, and the new one nominated by the Caliph Marwān, called Ibn Harashī, fought against each other for four months. They now made common cause against the Khawārij but were defeated by them in Rajab 127 (April 745) and had to vacate Kūfa. Ibn Harashī went back to Syria while Ibn ʿUmar returned to the fortified city of Wāsiṭ. In Shaʿbān 127 (May 745) Ḍaḥḥāk b. Qays followed him there and besieged him. The Kalbite Mansūr b. Jumhur distinguished himself in the fighting against the Khawārij but he was still the first to run over to them and undergo their inquisition as he promised to embrace Islam and to obey God's word. After some hesitation at the end of Shawwāl 127 (beginning of August 745), Ibn ʿUmar also crept out of his hole and gave the oath of allegiance to Ḍaḥḥāk b. Qays. A Qurayshite of the ruling family now prayed behind a Khārijite of Bakr b. Wā'il! And he was not the only one, for another Umayyad soon followed his example, as we shall see. One can understand the amazement at how times had changed, expressed in the verses transmitted in Ṭabarī II, p.1913, for example. In addition, Ibn ʿUmar was quite happy to remain as Governor of the Khārijites in Wāsiṭ and to govern the eastern half of his kingdom. He turned towards Kūfa, wishing to rule the western half from there. However, events called him to Moṣul and in Dhū 'l Qaʿda 127 he left Kūfa to go there. This at least is the account given by Abū ʿUdayda, from whom this report about the appearance of Ḍaḥḥāk in the year

127 is essentially taken (Ṭab.II, pp.1900ss., pp.1904ss., pp.1913ss.).

However, the dating of Ḍaḥḥāk's departure in Dhū 'l-Qa'da 127 (Ṭab.II, p.1914, l.16) leaves room for doubt. It is closely connected with the other statement (p.1913, l.13) that by Dhū 'l-Qa'da 127, Marwān had finished with Ḥimṣ and Syria and then had a free hand against Ḍaḥḥāk; this is false, anticipating events by nearly a year. According to Ṭabarī II, p.1938, l.19, Ḍaḥḥāk withdrew to his homeland, not then in the same year in which he had marched out but only after an absence of twenty months.

For the subsequent events 'Abd al-Wahhāb (on the authority of Abū Hāshim) in Ṭab.II, pp.1938ss. is the most important authority. The inhabitants of Moṣul summoned Ḍaḥḥāk from Kūfa; he came and drove away the Government representative. All flocked to him because he gave very high pay. His army is supposed to have grown to 120,000 men.[7] The son of the dead Caliph Hishām, that restless condottiere Sulaymān, joined him with his troop of 4,000 men. As Marwān himself was still besieging Ḥimṣ in Syria, he commissioned his son 'Abdalla whom he had left behind in the Mesopotamian residence city of Ḥarrān, to prevent Ḍaḥḥāk from making any further advance (out of Moṣul). 'Abdalla came to Nisibis but there he had to halt after a disastrous battle and was obliged to withdraw behind the walls of the city. Ḍaḥḥāk besieged him there.

His attempt to seize the Raqqa ford over the Euphrates by means of a corps which he detached, did not succeed. In the meantime, Marwān had finally overcome Ḥimṣ and now marched forth in person via Raqqa against Ḍaḥḥāk. The armies met at Kafartuta; Ḍaḥḥāk, who used to expose himself recklessly, was killed in a preliminary skirmish. His successor Khaybarī renewed the attack after a pause, broke through into the enemy camp but was overwhelmed there and was clubbed to death by the slaves in the camp. That took place in 128/745, probably towards the end of the year. Whilst Abū Mikhnaf (Ṭab.II, p.1913s., p.1938, p.1940) gives only a brief summary, Theophanes (A.M.6236s.) agrees in essence with the description of 'Abd al-Wahhāb. According to him, Ḍaḥḥāk rebelled in the year 127/744 in Iraq. In the following year, he appeared with an enormous force in Mesopotamia. At first Marwān sent his son against him but, after he had taken Ḥimṣ after a four-month long siege, he himself went to Mesopotamia and killed the rebel.

The Khawārij were still 40,000 strong and they now made the Yashkūrite Shaybān b. ʿAbd al-ʿAzīz (Abū Dulaf) their Caliph. On the advice of Sulaymān, this man led them back to the eastern bank of the Tigris opposite Moṣul. They held the city in their power and were linked with it by a pontoon bridge. Marwān set up camp opposite on the right bank. In this way he spent long months (of the year 129/746) without gaining any decisive success. But after his military commander, Ibn Hubayra, had wrested Kūfa from Khārijite rule,[8] he ordered him to send an army in support. As the Khawārij did not succeed in repelling this army, they abandoned their position at Moṣul, again on Sulaymān's advice, so as not to come between two fires, and marched via Ḥulwān to Ahwāz and Fārs where they joined the Jaʿfarid Ibn Muʿāwiya (Ṭab.II, p.1977). Pursued there by the enemy, finally they scattered. Sulaymān led his followers over the sea to India. Shaybān went to the east coast of Arabia and finally was slain in the year 134/751,[9] in the battle with the prince of ʿUmān, a member of the old pre-Islamic dynasty of the Banū Julanda.

---

1. Ibn Qutayba, p.209. The Khawārij generally practised the cult of martyrs. (Ṭab.II, p.900)

2. Ṭab.II, pp.1897s. As well as the Ṣufrites (II, p.1900, l.5, p.1901, l.10) there were also Bayhasites (p.1897, l.20).

3. As a soldier he was known by the name of Kuthāra (Ṭab.II, p.1625, l.15) and drew a pension of 1/6 dirham per day. He ordered some vinegar to be bought, instead of which he got wine, but he could not persuade the hawker to exchange it and could not get the magistrate to whom he complained to intervene. That was the cause of his wrath and, after he had formed his band, he first of all killed the magistrate in question.

4. Jabbul is the old Jambul in the Tigris marshes. It is often mentioned, for example, in the stories of the Zanj revolt. (See Le Strange: Lands of the Eastern Caliphate Cambridge 1930, p.38 - Ed.)

5. These are the Khārijites who seized control of Armenia and Adharbayjān and maintained possession of it against Marwān. So relates Baladhurī, p.209. Ṭabarī and Ibn al-Athīr say nothing of this. cf. Weil I, p.690.

6. See p.41, note 4.

7. The number is naturally based on popular estimates. But also according to Theophanes A.M. 6237, Ḍaḥḥāk was meta pleistēs dunameōs.

8. According to Abū Mikhnaf in Ṭabarī II, p.1946, this was in Ramaḍān 129/746. That is however somewhat too late.

9. Thus according to Ṭabarī III, p.78; cf. Ṭab. II, p.1945 (ʻAbd al-Wahhāb), p.1949 (Abū ʻUbayda), p.1979 (Madāʼinī). Abū Mikhnaf in Ṭab.II, 1948, says that Shaybān b. ʻAbd al-ʻAzīz was already killed in the year 130/747 in Sijistān. Perhaps he confuses him with the Ḥarūrite Shaybān b. Salama, who played a role in Khurāsān at the same time and who, in fact, was killed in 130/747, certainly not in Sijistān but in Sarakhs.

CHAPTER 12.

This widespread revolt which took place in particularly favourable circumstances had led the Khawārij nearer to the hegemony than any other of their actions. But it had also been the cause of their access to or alliance with foreign elements, according to the motto: "Whoever is not against us, is on our side". That was a political sentiment but not particularly Khārijite. Politically much less significant, but much more clearly Khārijite, was a somewhat later movement in Arabia, the last in the time of the Umayyads. In Ṭabarī, the chief source of information for the movement is an otherwise unknown commentator: Harūn b. Mūsā.[1] He also appears in the long article of Aghānī, vol.XX, pp.96ss., but alongside Madā'inī who gives a much more detailed account.[2]

Ibāḍites from Baṣra had sown the seeds of their propaganda in Southern Arabia.[3] In Haḍramaut, ʻAbdalla b. Yaḥyā, a Kindite of the Banū Shayṭān, was in touch with them. He felt that he could no longer look on at the reigning injustice. He was encouraged to revolt by the Baṣrans, from where he was joined by some prominent party companions, amongst them Balj b. ʻUyayna al-Asadī[4] and Abū Ḥamza Mukhtār b. Aws al-Azdī. The latter was ʻAbdalla's right hand man and in fact was more important than ʻAbdalla himself. At the beginning of 129/746, ʻAbdalla received the oath of allegiance as Caliph. He adopted the title of Ṭālib al-ḥaqq (Seeker of the Truth). His enemies called him The One-Eyed Man, perhaps because through this sign he was characterized as the Anti-Christ (Agh.XX, p.108, l.24). He gained the upper-hand in Haḍramaut, then crossed over to Yemen and overthrew the governor there[5] and in the second half of the year 129/746 (Agh. p.97, l.21, p.98, l.24) made his entry into the capital Ṣanʻā. There he organised his administration but, along with the change, he took the former officials under his protection, showed himself to be of mild disposition and evidently won over the hearts of the Yemenīs. He stressed that between the Khārijite way and orthodox Islam there was basically no difference. He only took a serious view of those vices for which the Qur'ān enjoins punishment but which were still in fashion. Many Khawārij from other regions flocked to him. At the end of the year 129/746, as the time of the Pilgrimage came round, he sent an army to Mecca under the command of Abū Ḥamza. It consisted of some 1,000 men who wore black and red turbans.[6] The official leader of the ceremony, the Umayyad ʿAbd al-Waḥīd b. Sulaymān b. ʿAbd al-Malik, the Governor of Medīna, put up no opposition to them but, for the duration of the festival, made a truce with them and returned to Medīna. But from there he despatched an army against them, led by the Umayyad ʿAbd al-ʿAzīz b. ʿAbdalla b. ʿAmr b. ʿUthmān.[7] 8,000 men are supposed to have marched out, a motley throng of most unwarlike appearance. There were many Qurayshites there, in magnificent dress. They considered the affair as a pleasant walk. The Umayyads particularly, who were still numerous in Medīna, were extremely arrogant in what they said about that rabble, as they imagined the Khawārij to be. Abū Ḥamza turned against the Medīnans and clashed with them near Qudayd on Thursday, 9th Ṣafar, 130.[8] He tried to show them in a friendly way that they actually should make common cause with him against the Umayyad hegemony. Only when they attacked and one of his people was wounded by an arrow, did he deem it permissible to shed their blood. He put them miserably to flight, but forbade any pursuit. Only against the Qurayshites, the true representatives of ungodly government, did he exercise no restraint whatsoever. Their corpses littered the field of battle, amongst them that of their leader ʿAbd al-ʿAzīz. Their prisoners were executed if they did not condescend to deny their descent. Thus it was that Qudayd became so notorious, but otherwise the blood-letting of those haughty dignitaries, who usually allowed others to snatch the chestnuts out of the fire, was regarded with approval. The way to Medīna now lay open to Abū Ḥamza and he made his way into the city on the 13th Ṣafar (23 October, 747) without any sword-play, after the Governor ʿAbd al-Waḥīd had vacated it.[9]

He remained for about three months in Medīna. Although he was a skilled soldier, he was also, by education, a scholar and preacher. A collection seems to have been made[10] of the speeches which he gave from the Prophet's pulpit, from which Harūn has included many, sometimes very extensive, specimens in his account. He described with trenchant examples the difference between the present government and that of the Prophet and the first two Caliphs. He thought that the Medīnans, in accordance with all their past history of enmity against the Umayyads, must of necessity agree with the Khawārij but that they did not draw the practical conclusion and did not help to bring down the unlawful government. He contrasted them with their forefathers, who willingly adopted the Prophet, although he had the whole world against him, with only young people and unknown figures on his side. The self-same considerations which now they raised against the Khawārij, were then raised against Muḥammad by the Meccans. Such words were heard not unwillingly. Abū Ḥamza did not only invoke the name of Islam against the government but also he stressed its moral claims on individuals: "Whosoever asserts that God gives commandments which cannot be adhered to, is God's and our enemy!" In particular he inveighed against whoring and drinking. He admired ʿUmar I because he had inflicted the prescribed punishment of flogging in eighty cases of wine-drinking, without regard for persons. The Medīnans were less understanding about that: their city was considered as the most licentious in the area of Islam. Although they recognized that Abū Ḥamza ruled lawfully and benevolently, the majority of them remained cool and rejected him. For all that, some of them were won over to his side: among them were not only poor people such as the pious Qur'ān reader and grammarian ʿAbd al-ʿAzīz Bishkast, an Iranian by birth, but also a great-grandson of the Caliph ʿUmar and a grandson of his equally highly distinguished son ʿAbdalla, namely Abū Bakr. b. Muḥammad. (Ṭab.II, p.2021, l.9).

In order to put down this revolt, the Umayyads had to rely again on the Syrians. Around the beginning of Jumādā I, 130/747, four thousand of them, mainly Qaysites, marched against Medīna, led by ʿAbd al-Malik Ibn ʿAtīya of the Saʿad Hawāzin.[11] As they had done previously on a similar occasion under Yazīd I, they claimed suitable compensation for the pangs of conscience caused by the task which lay before them - that of defiling the holy city. It is alleged that each one got 100 gold dīnārs, an

Arab horse and a baggage mule. The Khawārij, led by Abū Ḥamza, awaited them in Wādī 'l-Qurā. They were defeated and for the most part massacred in the middle of Jumādā I, 130 (21 January 748). Abū Ḥamza escaped with thirty men and fled to Mecca.[12] When Ibn ʿAtiya came to Medīna, he found everything there already in order. The Medīnans themselves had already dealt with the few remaining Khawārij who had been left behind (under Mufaḍḍal), and they killed the innocent helpless Bishkast when they received news of the result of the battle on the following Monday (Agh.XX, p.109, l.10). In Mecca Abū Ḥamza tried once more to hit back but, as he was unwilling to use strong measures to protect himself from the treachery of the inhabitants, his opposition was in vain. Ibn ʿAtiya was victorious once more: he had the prisoners executed and their fallen leaders (with Abū Ḥamza amongst them) crucified. After a longer stay in Ṭā'if, he then went to attack the Caliph Ṭālib al-Ḥaqq himself, defeated and killed him, and after a short siege, took his capital of Ṣanʿā and also brought Ḥaḍramaut into submission.[13] At the end of 130/747, he wished to return hastily to Mecca with a small escort, for the Caliph had charged him to lead the Pilgrimage, but on the way he was set upon and killed by two Murādites, sons of Jumāna, who took him for a robber.

Finally, we learn of a milder species of Khawārij (Ibāḍites), who, despite their purity and severity, did not try to slaughter the Catholic Muslims, but to win them over to their side. Their defeat followed on the heels of the demise of the Umayyad kingdom.

---

1. Written Hārūn in Ṭab. and Harūn in Agh. (Ed.)

2. Harūn's Nisba (Ṭab.II, p.1942, l.14, p.1981, l.12, Agh.XX, p.98, l.29) is written differently every time. The following passages derive from him: Agh. p.98, ll.29-100, l.23 = Ṭab.II, p.1942s., pp.1981ss., pp.2006s., and Agh. p.103, l.21 - p.105, l.2 = Ṭab. p.2008 - 2011. Only Ṭab. p.2012ss. gives the concluding account; in Aghānī there are only some variants inserted into another context. But in its place in Agh.XX, pp.105-108, much greater space than in Ṭabarī is accorded to the Khārijite sermons

which Harūn repeats with delight. Therefore the author of Aghānī cannot, as he would have one believe, (p.98, 1.29, p.103, 1.21), have derived his knowledge of Harūn from Ṭabarī. That is also impossible on other grounds. The threads of the account which Ṭabarī more often than not breaks and then picks up again, are unbroken in his account and lack Ṭabarī's attempts at patching up. Also, the tenor of his version is here and there more complete, as a comparison of Aghānī p.99, 1.19s. with Ṭab.II, 1982, 1.10 shows in particular. In the Leiden edition of Ṭabarī, several mistakes could have been corrected from Aghānī, and lacunae filled in. From Madā'inī the following passages are derived: Agh. p.97, 1.1 - p.98, 1.2; p.100, 1.24 - p.103, 1.20; p.108, 1.8 - p.114, 1.15. In the account of the last passage, several variants to Harūn are noted, (p.106, p.110), as we have said. Two short traditions of Wāqidī are found in Ṭabarī II, p.2008, p.2012.

3. According to an approved practice, they used the Ḥajj to Mecca to prepare their principles (Ṭab.II, p.1942). Already in the year 107/725, ʿAbbād al-Ruʿaynī had incited a Khārijite revolt in Yemen, (Ṭab.II, p.1487).

4. Thus his name is quoted in Ṭabarī, II, p.2012, 1.10; the Patronym is given differently in Agh.XX, p.97,1.14, and likewise the nisba which, however, is written incorrectly there.

5. From the family Abū ʿAqil who rose to fortune through al-Ḥajjāj and who had reigned in Yemen for half a century.

6. Agh.XX, p.99, 1.8, p.112, 1.31. Wāqidī in Ṭabarī II, p.2008 gives the number as only around 400.

7. This was his name according to Harūn (Agh.XX, p.100, 1.6) and Wāqidī (Ṭab.II, p.2009, 1.2). Madā'inī (Agh. p.100, 1.25) calls him ʿAbd al-ʿAzīz b. ʿUmar b. ʿAbdalazīz; but afterwards (p.101, 1.14) he says himself that he was a descendant of the Caliph ʿUthmān. He has therefore made a mistake, if it does not result from the hand of a copyist. Also he is

probably wrong in that he makes ʻAbd al-Waḥīd the Governor of Mecca, and ʻAbd al- Azīz the Governor of Medīna.

8. Thursday, 19 October, 747. The accounts vary between 7th and 9th Ṣafar (Agh. p.101, 1.16, Ṭab.II, p.2009, 1.1). Thursday decides in favour of the figure 9, which quite frequently is confused with the figure 7.

9. The date given in Ṭabarī II, p.2012, 1.4. Madā'inī always has Balj to the fore; he gives the impression (Agh.XX, p.102, 1.14) that after the Battle of Qudayd Abū Ḥamza returned to Mecca, although subsequently (p.108, 11.5ss.) he also has him still in Medīna. Besides Balj many other officers of Abū Ḥamza were named, for example, Abraha b. Ṣabbāḥ from a leading Kindite family and Ibn Ḥusayn from a leading Ḥārithite family. One sees from this that distinguished Yemenīs took part in the revolt and not merely a collection of poor folk as is usually reported.

10. Edited by the Grammarian Ibn Faḍāla (Agh.XX, p.105, 1.27). The Grammarians also busied themselves with the pulpit speeches of Ziyād and al-Ḥajjāj. A collection of sermons by Ṣāliḥ b. Musarrih is mentioned earlier. Not only the Khawārij but also the Shīʻites cultivated this type of literature. They memorized the speeches of their leaders who were all very much of the same type and wrote them down by and by. (Ṭab.II, p.500, 1.1, p.508, 1.13). Then along came the philologists and polished them up somewhat.

11. cf. for what follows Agh. vol.XI, pp.83ss. There the full name of ʻAbd al-Malik is given; ʻAtiya was his great-grandfather.

12. Here, I have tried to make the varying reports of Harūn and Madā'inī agree. Madā'inī again puts Balj in the fore-front, he being killed at Wādī'l-Qurā.

13. A long elegy on the slain leaders of the Ibāḍiya, quoting their names, is given in Agh.XX, pp.111s. Further verses are those in which Maryam, the wife of Abū Ḥamza, went forth

to meet death in battle (p.109, l.27s.) and scornful verses about the unfortunate Bishkast (p.110, l.20s.). The victory songs of Abū Ṣa<u>kh</u>r (p.108, l.20ss., p.111, l.5ss.) are missing from the Dīwān of Hu<u>dh</u>ayl.

2 - THE SHĪ'A

CHAPTER 1.

With the murder of ʿUthmān, Islam split up into two parties,[1] under ʿAlī and Muʿāwiya. "Party" is the meaning of the Arabic word Shīʿa, the Shīʿa of ʿAlī thus was opposed to a Shīʿa of Muʿāwiya. But after Muʿāwiya became the ruler of the whole kingdom and was no longer merely at the head of a party, the word Shīʿa was applied simply to the followers of ʿAlī, implying at the same time their opposition to the Khawārij. But ʿAlī was not elected leader because he was the cousin and son-in-law of the Prophet and the father of his grandsons. The right of succession to the ruling position within an immediate family as though it were its private property, carried no weight amongst the Arabs and is certainly not lawful in Islam.[2] He was chosen much more because he appeared the worthiest of the oldest companions of Muḥammad, from amongst whom until then the Caliph always emerged; they had supported him as they had the Prophet himself in a sort of council of state,[3] and, as it were, maintained the continuity of theocratic government alongside the changes of those who occupied the highest position. Thus he was originally the representative of this circle of worthy Islamic dignitaries and their firmly established right to rule the Theocracy, a right which was badly threatened by the temporal power of the Umayyads - an old Qurayshite aristocracy with pre-Islamic heathen traditions, who had been awarded all the official positions by ʿUthmān. As soon as ʿAlī came to the fore, the few remaining members of the religious aristocracy who had promoted his cause until then turned against him. They placed the blame incurred by the murder of ʿUthmān upon him and, at the same time, claimed the benefits of the deed for themselves. The power struggle was in fact waged by all the pretenders to the ruling position, and the law was only here and there a pretext in order to lure the masses and provide them with a watchword. But ʿAlī managed to keep the Iraqis firmly on his side, as they were the most important source of support for the revolutionary groups in the rising against ʿUthmān. He changed his residence to Kūfa and afterwards won over Baṣra in addition, but only after a bloody encounter with his treacherous rivals.

Muʿāwiya had Syria behind him, the province which he had administered for a long time. The struggle between him and ʿAlī was transformed into a struggle between Syria and Iraq. With ʿAlī's death, the tide turned against the Iraqis and they became part of the united kingdom which Muʿāwiya created, but only under coercion and certainly not with any sincerity. Thenceforth, ʿAlī became the symbol of their opposition to the Syrian yoke. They looked back upon that brief time as a golden age, when Kūfa and not Damascus had been the capital of Islam, containing the central state treasury. The Shīʿa therefore became established in Iraq where they were originally not a sect but the political expression of the whole province. In this sense, one may as well say that all native Iraqis, particularly in Kūfa, were more or less Shīʿite, not merely as individuals but also as tribes with their tribal leaders.[4] They were distinguished only by differences of degree. ʿAlī represented for them the lost ruling glory of their homeland.[5] For that reason only arose a veneration of his person and his family which he had not enjoyed during his lifetime. Already at an early date, a veritable cult of him was begun within an obscure sect.

Abū Mikhnaf is the principal authority for the history of the Shīʿa, so long as it took place essentially in Kūfa. Ṭabarī follows almost exclusively his very detailed accounts.[6] After Muʿāwiya had subdued Iraq, he appointed the Thaqafite Mughīra b. Shuʿba as governor in Kūfa. He left him in most respects a completely free hand, but demanded that he should curse ʿAlī from the minbar every Friday during the Friday prayer and that he should ensure the presence there of some particularly zealous and devoted companions of ʿAlī whom Muʿāwiya named. Amongst them was Ḥujr b. ʿAdī, an important member (although not the head) of the Kinda, who had distinguished himself on ʿAlī's side at Ṣiffīn and other occasions. He protested regularly on Fridays in the Mosque, shouting out that the curse would rebound upon the cursers. Mughīra warned him, but did him no harm. Towards the end of his life, as Mughīra once again was pronouncing the prescribed curse-formula, the bold Ḥujr shouted out: "You are a decrepit old man, give us our pensions which you withhold from us and then all will be well!" That met with general approbation. Mughīra came down from the minbar and went home. His Thaqafī companions reproached him, but he said: "I have no desire in my old age to lose my time in the Hereafter by shedding Muslim blood, so that Mu'āwiya may be secure in this life. Moreover, I have killed Ḥujr in all but deed because he will do the same thing to my successor and will be delivered to the knife."

With Mughīra's successor, Ḥujr did indeed fall upon the wrong person. It was Ziyād b. Abīh the Governor of Baṣra, who was also appointed to Kūfa in the year 51/671. We have no report from Abū Mikhnaf about his first appearance there. According to Madā'inī, he came with a small escort, mounted the minbar and commented favourably on the fact that there he found peace and order, and did not find it necessary to establish them as was the case in Baṣra. Those present thanked him for his praise by pelting him with gravel. But his men occupied the exits of the mosque and refused exit to any who would not swear that he had not joined in the stone-throwing. The few who were proud enough to refuse this oath had their hands cut off. This is a fine story which is often related in other places, but does not seem to have the ring of truth. At least 'Awāna, according to Ṭabarī, II, p.114, relates quite a different version. According to him, nothing happened when Ziyād first mounted the minbar in Kūfa. When he came to the end of the oath against 'Alī and pronounced the blessing upon 'Uthmān, no word of opposition was spoken. He turned peacefully home to Baṣra leaving behind the Qurayshite 'Amr b. Ḥurayth as his permanent representative in Kūfa. It was only against this man that the Shī'ites dared revolt, having become arrogant as a result of Mughīra's indulgence. Ḥujr b. 'Adī was at their head, and they threw stones at 'Amr during the Friday prayer. Thereupon Ziyād quickly returned from Baṣra, mounted the minbar in elegant dress and made those present aware of the seriousness of the situation as he threatened Ḥujr. Ḥujr himself was present in the mosque, but then departed with his followers.[7]

At this point Abū Mikhnaf in Ṭabarī takes up

the account again. Whilst still in the mosque, Ziyād began to act. First he turned his wrath against the Kūfan notables present, the Ashrāf: "You are present here with me but your brothers, your sons and cousins are with Ḥujr. If you do not prove that you are innocent by your actions, I shall bring the Syrians down upon you." This helped and each one of them hastened to bring his relatives home. The crowd which had gathered around Ḥujr on the market-place (beside the mosque) dispersed. The military police helped with blows of their clubs, while Ziyād looked on. Ḥujr himself was saved by the Kindite, Abū Amarrata, the only one of them who had a sword with him, with which he laid low a pursuer without actually killing him. Ḥujr reached his compound safely, where once again a crowd had gathered. Because the few military police did not seem to be sufficient, Ziyād ordered out the whole Kūfan army. But he kept the Muḍar beside him, on the square in front of the mosque. He sent only Yemenis[8] in pursuit, the group to which Ḥujr himself belonged. This was to prevent discord between them and the Muḍar in this delicate affair, and also to humiliate them because they were carrying out the tyrant's orders against their own tribal and political companions - for they were all Shīʿites at heart. However, the Kinda and those closely related to them, the Ḥaḍramaut, were not amongst the conscripts because the attack was directed against them, or at least against one of their people. The Azd co-operated with them, but only outwardly for appearance's sake. They went around excusing themselves from house to house as they entered the quarter of the Kinda. They allowed the Madhhij and Hamdān to go on ahead, and these two groups advanced unhindered to Ḥujr's compound. There they met with opposition. When he was attacked in his house, the Banū Jabala, his kinsmen, acted on his behalf; in addition he was supported by those who in other respects were not at all in agreement with him. He is supposed to have ordered them to put away their arms and to disperse. This would probably have happened without the order. He himself managed to escape and Ziyād had him pursued by the military police. He fled from compound to compound, street to street and quarter to quarter.[9] He was conducted by skilled guides through the confusion because general sympathy was on his side. He found admission where he sought it but did not want to test those who sheltered him too severely and so left as soon as his persecutors approached. Finally he found sanctuary in the house of an Azdite. The pursuers had lost his traces and abandoned the vain search. But now Ziyād made his tribe responsible for him and threatened the head of the Kinda, Muḥammad b. Ash'ath, with dreadful punishments if he did not produce the outlaw within three days. As a result of this, Ḥujr gave himself up voluntarily, after he had been promised that he would not be judged by Ziyād but would be sent to the Caliph. When he approached on a cold morning, wrapped in a burnous, he had not expected to be beaten about the head or to be thrown into prison. But his loud protest was in vain. For fifteen days he remained in jail. During this time Ziyād swiftly hunted down other Shī'ites who had severely compromised themselves and collected about a dozen of them. They were people of all tribes. They were in part betrayed by their kinsmen, or they gave themselves up. None of them agreed to deny 'Alī in front of Ziyād in order to escape retribution.

Ziyād now drew up an accusation of violent revolt against Ḥujr and his companions. The distinguished Kūfans hastened to add their signatures, to the extent that he had to send several of them away since seventy witnesses were sufficient for him. Some excused themselves afterwards or denied their signatures,[10] and the Qāḍī Shuraykh b. Hānī al-Ḥārithī revoked his before the Caliph. The text of the accusation was then handed over to the two military police who had to escort the prisoners to Mu'āwiya in Syria. One evening,[11] the sad procession set out: the 'Absite Qabīṣa saw how his daughters looked after him and he was permitted to take leave of them. No hand was raised to free the prisoners although it would have been easy. This fear on the part of the tribes before the supreme power of the state, before two policemen, wounded the prisoners more than their own danger of death. For them it was the downfall of their people. In a place before Damascus, known as the virgin meadow, a halt was made. The prisoners remained there in chains. Mu'āwiya received the text of the accusation and gave it more credence than the defence which Ḥujr raised through his messengers. Moreover, he consulted Ziyād again and held counsel with his true followers. On their recommendation, he allowed six of the prisoners to go free, but refused to allow the intercession of the Sakūnite Mālik b. Hubayra on behalf of Ḥujr himself. He offered pardon to Ḥujr and to the other prisoners if they would renounce ʿAlī. Two did so and saved their lives; this was also the case later when they went back on their denial. The remaining six were executed. Ḥujr broke out trembling when he saw the shroud spread out and the open grave and the drawn sword, but he remained firm. Mālik b. Hubayra came too late. Angered by the fact that Muʿāwiya had not wished to spare Ḥujr's life on his request, he appeared with the Kinda and the Sakūn on the virgin meadows in order to free the prisoners by force. But they were already dead. His anger against the Caliph subsided, when the latter sent him 100,000 dirhems, and he claimed, in addition, that by killing Ḥujr he had wanted to spare the trouble of a second campaign against the Iraqis - after the previous campaign in ʿAlī's lifetime and after his death - for Ḥujr would without doubt have dragged them into revolt. The executed were buried as good Muslims.[12]

In a short account of Ibn Kalbī, on the authority of Muḥammad b. Sīrīn, which Ṭabarī II, p.115s. reproduces, Ḥujr is portrayed as an innocent lamb led to the slaughter. His men wished to help him but he quietly allowed himself to be chained and led off to Syria: on hearing his friendly greeting Muʿāwiya said "Off with his head". He had no accomplices. The later shīʿite tendency appeared in Yaʿqūbī (II, pp.273ss.) in an even sillier form. Abū Mikhnaf remains firmly in sympathy with Ḥujr; he is supposed not to have wanted his followers to incite one power against the other, despite the fact that he had caused this to happen. However, the true facts of the case appear plainly in his account. The Shīʿite Abū Amarrata was the first to draw his sword and shed blood, whilst the military police only attacked with their clubs. Also ʿAbdalla b. Khalīfa al-Ṭāʾī fought bravely for Ḥujr (Ṭab.II, p.121, p.129). There is no doubt that Ḥujr was a rebel and would gladly have brought out the Kūfans with him. Ziyād, in our opinion, was quite correct and Muʿāwiya even acted mildly. But that age thought differently. The killing of a Muslim was only allowed and enjoined if he had killed another Muslim; this was by way of blood-revenge. As a rule the avenger was the one who performed the deed of vengeance, while the role of public authority was restricted to allowing him to do this. The only crime against the state was to break away from Islam and not high treason, unless it was connected with death and murder. Any execution carried out by the state, even if it was justified, caused the greatest agitation, especially in this first case when it was applied to very prominent men. For these reasons, the Kūfans felt generally humiliated. The Governor of Khurasān, Rabīʿ b. Ziyād is supposed to have broken his heart with grief, although he was not otherwise particularly susceptible to emotion. ʿĀisha also gave vent to her anger, just as the pious al-Ḥasan of Baṣra did at a later date, although he was not inspired by personal motives like the Mother of the Believers. Muʿāwiya is supposed to have suffered bitter pangs of conscience on his death-bed and to have justified himself by saying that he had been exposed to Ziyād's influence because the Quraysh had turned away from him. Naturally, it also involved the defiance of the government by the tribes, in particular the mighty Yemenīs, for they found it insulting that they could not save their members from the power of the state. But tribal opposition was united with religious opposition. The Shīʿites in particular were aroused by Ḥujr's execution. His martyrdom was the prelude to that of the principal Shīʿite martyr, Ḥusayn b. ʿAlī.

---

1. Wellhausen has prepared his account from historical sources. To these may be added the writings of the heresiographers: al-Baghdādī, al-Farq bayn al-Firaq; al-Nawbakhtī, Firaq al-Shīʿa; al-Shahrastānī, Kitāb al-Milal wa'l-Niḥal; al-Ashʿarī, Maqālāt al-Islāmiyīn; Ibn Ḥazm, al-Fiṣāl fī'l-Milal. (L)

2. Muhammad was succeeded by two sons-in-law and two fathers-in-law. Both the Umayyads and the ʿAbbāsids established dynasties. Succession within one family was not guaranteed in either Arab or Islamic mores, but a strong sentiment favoured it nonetheless. (L)

3. The so-called shūrā. (Ed.)

4. One can see this for example in the story about Mustawrid which is reproduced above, pp.29ss.

5. Kūfa was the real centre for support for ʿAlī. The Kūfan tribesmen were interested in the distribution of tax revenues and they opposed the centralizing tendencies of ʿUmar and ʿUthmān who insisted on keeping surplus revenues in the hands of the Caliphate. After ʿAlī's death, his family, as is clear below, had only scant support even in Kūfa. Wellhausen speaks loosely in calling Kūfan support for ʿAlī an Iraqi movement and defence of the homeland. (L)

6. See Ṭab.II, pp.109ss. (Ed.)

7. According to this therefore, Ḥujr's putsch occurred in the year in which Ziyād took over the governorship of Kūfa, that is 51/671. Contrary to that, according to Madāʾinī in Ṭab.II, p.162, it was only in the year of Ziyād's death, 53/672.

8. Curiously, no mention is made of the Rabīʿa. Amongst the Muḍar are quoted the Tamīm, Hawāzin, Bahīla (Aʿṣur), Asad and Ghaṭafān. Amongst the Yemen are (i) the Madhḥij and Hamdān; (ii) the Azd, Bajīla, Khathʿam, Anṣār, Khuzāʿa and Quḍāʿa. Besides these the Kinda and Ḥaḍramaut are included. The Anṣār, who are taken together with the Yemen, are not to be confused with the Ahl Medīna (= Ahl al-ʿĀliya, Ṭab.II, p.1382) who come only from the administrative area of Medīna and belong in fact to Muḍar. Under ʿUmar I, the Kūfans were divided into seven sections, only six of which are referred to in Ṭab.I, p.2495: (i) the Kināna with the Aḥābīsh and Jadīla; (ii) the Quḍāʿa (Ghassān b. Shibām), Bajīla, Khathʿam, Kinda, Ḥaḍramaut, Azd; (iii) the Madhḥij, Ḥimyar, Hamdān; (iv) the Tamīm with Ribāb and Hawāzin; (v) Asad, Ghaṭafān with Muḥārib, Namir, Ḍubayʿa (Bakr) and Taghlib; (vi) the Iyād, ʿAkk, ʿAbd al-Qays, Ahl Hajar, al-Ḥamrāʾ (Iranians). Ziyād arranged them into four quarters (Arbāʿ) in the following positions: (i) Ahl Medīna; (ii) Tamīm and Hamdān; (iii) Rabīʿa and Kinda; (iv) Madhḥij and Asad. Quite different tribes were contained together in these quarters, which were artificial unions (merely dictated by location?). They were of approximately similar strength with no tribal chiefs at their head, but Government appointed administrators

or leaders. The most powerful of the tribes was the combined Hamdān and Madhḥij.

9. The tribes lived in quarters, families in streets, and kinsmen together in compounds. The quarters bore the names of the tribes (Ḥujr fled from the Kinda, through the Nakhaʿ to the Azd) and the streets the names of the families. Thus the layout of Kūfa gave an insight into the ethnic genealogies of the Arabs. The same applied in Baṣra.

10. The names were not, or at least not all, actually written down in person by those who had supported Ziyād's accusation.

11. Times of day are often given - calendar dates are not!

12. cf. the verses of ʿAbdalla b. Khalīfa, Ṭab.II, pp.148-154; he appears to give the number of executed as eight, perhaps including the two who recanted. They were certainly spared by Muʿāwiya, but later were killed.

CHAPTER 2.

Ḥasan, the eldest son of ʿAlī by Fāṭima, had died in the year 49/669. He had disappointed his father's followers and had lost their respect by the base manner in which he renounced the ruling position. They then turned their eyes to his younger brother Ḥusayn. The vacancy of the Caliphate caused by the death of Muʿāwiya in the year 60/679, aroused fresh aspirations of the party. Ḥusayn, then a man in his mid-fifties, refused the oath of allegiance to Yazīd and, to avoid coercion, he fled from Medīna, the permanent home of the ʿĀlids, and found asylum in Mecca (end of Rajab 60/679). The Kūfans invited him to come to lead a revolt against Umayyad rule. With this in mind, they wrote many letters to him: the first messengers reached Mecca on 10 Ramaḍān, 60 (14th June, 680). Zealous Shīʿites like Sulaymān b. Ṣurād al-Khuzāʿī went there, followed by others. Prominent men from all the tribes were amongst the letter-signatories,[1] but chiefly the Yemenīs, who were generally dominant in Kūfa in number and significance. Ḥusayn indicated that he was ready to comply with the urgent summons voiced from all sides. But first he sent a scout, his cousin Muslim b. ʿĀqil, to seek out the lie of the land and to prepare the way for him. Muslim stayed in Kūfa first, with the Thaqafī Mukhtār b. Abī ʿUbayd,[2] but afterwards he settled down with the distinguished Muradite Hānī b. ʿUrwa of the Madhḥij. His place of residence remained secret, although meetings were held there and mighty speeches made. Recruitment for Ḥusayn's cause was energetic, although it went on with great prudence and not every man who reported was immediately accepted. However, within a very short time, thousands gave the oath of allegiance to Muslim or his true followers. Abū Thumāma al-Ṣāʿidī gathered money and weapons. Everything seemed so favourable that Muslim sent instructions to Ḥusayn that he only had to come.

The Governor of Kūfa on Muslim's arrival was the Anṣārī Nuʿmān b. Bashīr. He was well aware that something was going on but feared to apply preventive punishments on mere suspicion: his duty to God took precedence over that to his secular master. As soon as the Caliph Yazīd learnt of his behaviour, on the advice of Serjius, he replaced him with the less scrupulous ʿUbaydalla b. Ziyād of Baṣra.[3] This man hurried by the shortest route through the desert to Kūfa with only a small escort.[4] Riding in with a black turban and veiled mouth, he was at first taken for Ḥusayn, whom they were expecting.[5] When he revealed his identity, the citadel was most willingly vacated for him. Then he immediately introduced himself in the mosque and gave a short speech. He bound over every ʿarīf[6] to denounce every stranger in his ʿirāfa, or to vouch that there was no suspicious person living in it. Otherwise he would be crucified before the entrance to his compound, his ʿirāfa deprived of the pension, and he would be banished from Kūfa.

Already in Baṣra, ʿUbaydalla b. Ziyād had had authentic news of Ḥusayn's intention as a result of an intercepted letter, but he seems to have known nothing[7] of Muslim's presence in Kūfa, or at all events nothing of his place of residence. Unsuspectingly, he went into the lion's den, into the house of Hānī b. ʿUrwa in order to visit a sick person there. His life hung upon a thread.[8] The ʿurafāʾ reported nothing. Only a spy put him on the track, not a pure-blooded Arab but a mawlā named Maʿqil. This man gained secret access to the Shīʿite Ibn ʿAwsaja. He showed him 3,000 dirhams which he had collected for the party and would willingly hand over to the right man. Through Ibn ʿAwsaja he was introduced to Muslim and admitted to the oath of allegiance. Thenceforth he was always around him. He heard and saw everything which went on in the compound of Hānī b. ʿUrwa and then reported it to ʿUbaydalla.

ʿUbaydalla now had Hānī brought to him by two noblemen whom he had befriended, on the pretext that he had not seen him for such a long time. As soon as he appeared, he was interrogated.[9] Confronted by the spy, he retracted his denial and promised to send away his guest. But he refused to hand him over and when ʿUbaydalla threatened him with death, he said: "In that case the swords of the Madhḥij would gleam about your dwelling!" In reply, ʿUbaydalla struck him in the face with his club so that blood flowed. He thereupon snatched at the sword of a guard who was standing close by, then he was seized and imprisoned. Meanwhile, the Ma<u>dh</u>ḥij actually had appeared before the citadel, crying out: "We do not wish to disturb the peace, only we have heard that our brother is in danger of death!" They were appeased by the re-assurance of the timid Qāḍī Shuray<u>kh</u> that Hānī was still alive, thanked God, and withdrew as though everything was all right.

However ʻUbaydalla was still not out of danger. On hearing the news of Hānī's arrest, Muslim decided to wait no longer. With the supporters whom he had quickly gathered together,[10] he proceeded on that very day to the market-place. ʻUbaydalla had just time to get out of the mosque in which he had led the prayers and to escape into the citadel which stood close by. He had only a few freed-men and thirty police on hand. But also he had the support of the <u>Ashrāf</u>, twenty of the most distinguished Kūfans: they were, in his power, although to some extent zealous Shīʻites who had participated in the summoning of Ḥusayn.[11] They had to warn those who had banded together of the evil consequences of their action and to prevail upon them to change. Also the women detained their relatives saying: "You have no business there, and will not be missed." Towards evening the crowd did indeed disperse and Muslim was quite isolated. He wandered around because he had no knowledge of the twisting streets of Kūfa and finally found shelter with one of the widows who lived amongst the Banū Jabala (of Kinda); she was standing in front of her door waiting for her son.

At nightfall, when the market-place had become quite still, ʻUbaydalla ordered the <u>Ashrāf</u> to see whether the coast was clear. They climbed up on to the colonnades running round the mosque and illuminated the scene by hanging lanterns from the upper windows. There was nobody to be seen any more. Then he dared to come down from the citadel into the mosque and ordered everyone to attend the late evening prayer. The Kūfans came in their masses; they were put into military formation and drawn up in these positions through the night. The military police were all deployed and had to occupy all the exits of the streets so that they could search the individual quarters next day. But at day-break, the son of the widow revealed Muslim's hiding-place to the tribal leader of the Kinda, Muḥammad b. Ash'ath, and from him further to the governor. Ibn Ash'ath ordered that he be brought to him. He took along some police and 60 to 70 Qaysites, for Yemenīs would never have found the fugitive. After strong resistance - they wanted to capture him alive - finally Muslim surrendered to Ibn Ash'ath and was led away on a mule, after his sword had been confiscated. On entering the citadel he demanded a drink, but nobody moved to fulfil his request until finally a Qurayshite took pity on him. After a sharp exchange of words with 'Ubaydalla, he received the death-sentence. 'Umar b. Sa'ad b. Abī Waqqāṣ, the son of one of the oldest companions of Muḥammad, only agreed to receive his last will and testament on the advice of the governor of the city. He was then led to one of the turrets of the citadel and there was decapitated by a Persian military policeman whom he had wounded in the battle. The torso was cast down on to what became subsequently the Butcher's market.

Then it was Hānī's turn: the intercession of the Ashrāf did not help him. With hands bound behind his back, he was led to the market-place. He shouted out for his tribe, but nobody listened. Then he burst his bonds and sought for a weapon, but it was in vain. He was unwilling to stretch out his neck: "Must I then help you to kill me?". Finally he fell under the blows of a Turkish freedman. One or two others were executed inside the tribal quarters themselves, as an act of defiance to the tribes. The heads of the two chief offenders were sent by 'Ubaydalla to the Caliph Yazīd, along with a short letter which he had composed with his own hand, for he did not like the long elegantly written epistle of his scribe, 'Amr b. Nāfi', who wished to introduce the verbose Persian style. Yazīd approved his action, only stipulating that he should not kill anyone who had not taken arms against him.

About a month before his death Muslim had written to Ḥusayn saying that he should come. On the same day on which Muslim revolted in Kūfa, Ḥusayn is supposed to have left Mecca on 8th Dhū'l-Ḥijja, 60.[12] People waited for the imminent event in an atmosphere of tension, and the pious son of the old heathen 'Amr b. 'Āṣ went so far as to pronounce oracles about it. Whilst Ibn al-Zubayr had wanted to get the Prophet's grandson out of Mecca,[13] those who were favourably inclined towards him dissuaded him. But he would not listen to them and off he went on his way. His closest relatives followed him, with women and children, and also the sons of ʿAbdalla b. Jaʿfar, but there were no ʿAbbāsids. In Tanʿīm, he seized one of the caravans destined for the Caliph - the camels proved useful to him. Then he went along the road to Kūfa and travelled via Dhāt Irq, Hājir in the Wādī Dhū'l-Rumma, Zarūd and Thaʿlabīya to Zubāla. A few Kūfans, who were returning from the pilgrimage, joined him. They did so with reluctance and only when requested, but subsequently they kept faith with him. Some of the Bedouin from the watering places at which he camped followed him. He thought he would be received in Kūfa with open arms and still knew nothing of Muslim's sad fate. The first news reached him in Thaʿlabīya. He would willingly have turned back there and then if the brothers of the slain man on whom lay the duty of revenge had allowed it. In Zubāla he received further bad news. One of his messengers, by whom he had wished to be announced in Kūfa, was imprisoned by Ḥusayn b. Tamīm[14] who was stationed in Qādisiya. On the command of the governor, the messenger was hurled down from the citadel because he refused to renounce his lord and master. On hearing this report, he allowed his followers to disperse and the Bedouin took advantage of this. He himself went on further with those who remained faithful, via Baṭn ʿAqaba and Sharāf to the oasis of Dhū Husam, where he pitched his tents, being protected in the rear by the nature of the terrain.

There his path was blocked by Kūfan cavalry who had been sent from Qādisiya led by the Tamīmite Ḥurr b. Yazīd. Moreover, they treated him with respect and performed the prayer under his direction. He showed them the letters which he had received from Kūfa, two bags full; however they made clear that they wanted no part of that. He now wished to return to Medīna itself. Ḥurr could not allow him to do that, but still had no orders to attack. So he proposed that he should choose a way which led neither to Medīna nor to Kūfa, until he, Ḥurr, received written instructions from the governor to whom he had to report. Accordingly, Ḥusayn set out west of Udhayb and Qādisiya. Ḥurr remained constantly by his side but did not prevent sincere individual Kūfan Shī'ites from joining him. They told him that the Ashrāf had been won over by the government, and that the remaining Kūfans were for him in their hearts but would fight against him with their swords.

The journey continued further via Udhayb al-Hijānāt and Qaṣr Banī Muqātil towards Nīnawā on the Euphrates. There Ḥurr got instructions from 'Ubaydalla that he had to allow Ḥusayn no rest, nor let him camp in any citadel or oasis. He acted accordingly. Ḥusayn could not establish himself in Nīnawā or Ghādirīya or Shāfi'a. He did not follow the advice to attack the few cavalry under Ḥurr, being unwilling to start the fighting. "You have only to go to that village on the Euphrates, then the others will begin". But that village was called 'Aqr, and the unlucky name scared him off. He remained in a water-less position close to the Euphrates, on the plain of Kerbelā.[15] It was, according to Ṭabarī, II, p.308, l.7, on Thursday 2nd. Muḥarram, 61 (Tuesday, 2nd October, 680).

On the following morning, 'Umar b. Sa'ad b. Abī Waqqāṣ appeared on the scene with four thousand Kūfans. The province of Rayy had been assigned to him by 'Ubaydalla so that he could campaign against the Daylamites in Dastaba. He had assembled the army for this reason, but now he got the order to conquer Ḥusayn first. Unwillingly, he obeyed, so as not to lose his province. However, he was in no hurry to act. First he had Ḥusayn asked what exactly he wanted. With difficulty he found a messenger to go to him, for most of the distinguished men in his army had previously written to Ḥusayn and therefore were ashamed to appear before him. Ḥusayn said that he had been summoned by the Kūfans but, since the Kūfans had changed their minds, he begged to be allowed to return.[16] 'Umar transmitted this message to the Governor. 'Ubaydalla replied that Ḥusayn had to accept the oath of allegiance to Yazīd and to yield. Otherwise, he would be attacked immediately. If 'Umar refused to do this, he would have to hand over command to the Qaysite Shamir b. Dhī'l-Jawshān,[17] his messenger who brought the reply.

In the evening of 9 Muḥarram,[18] 'Umar made preparations to attack. During the night Ḥusayn was left in peace. None of his followers took advantage of the period to flee, although Ḥusayn asked them to, as only he himself was wanted. He made his will, and had his sword made ready thereby terrifying the women, and gave orders that they should secure themselves from attack in the rear.[19] He spent the rest of the night in prayer. The enemy stood near at hand in front of his tents and conversations were held back and forth from place to place.

On the 10th Muḥarram, 61,(Wednesday[20], the 10th October, 680) after the early morning prayer, the parties took up their positions. On Ḥusayn's side there were only 70 men, including his eighteen cousins, with 32 horses.[21] It was a heart-warming event for him when, at the twelfth hour, Ḥurr b. Yazīd came to join him and was ready to die for him, so making amends for his earlier behaviour. Words preceded the battle. Ḥusayn made a speech to the enemy from high upon his camel. An arrow, which however did not wound him, put an end to that. Exchanges of arrows were followed by skirmishes with swords. Ḥusayn's true followers took leave of him vowing to meet him in Paradise, before they went one after another into this last fight. They had no other object than to die before his eyes. He sat in front of the largest tent which sheltered the lamenting women and children, and surveyed the fighting from there. Furthermore, his cousins seem to have behaved as spectators until the others had shed their blood, and their turn came. Then they were all slain. But nobody dared to attack the Prophet's grandson, until Shamir ended the delay. He was the leader of the attack, if however one can speak of a leader. He managed to separate Ḥusayn from the tent containing the women and children, which was regarded as sacred. Now several men fell upon him and killed him, with 33 thrusts and 34 cuts to the body. Afterwards, according to the circumstances, nobody or everybody wanted to be the murderer. The corpse was undressed, one took the trousers, another the shirt, the silken burnous, the shoes and the sword - Ḥusayn wore a ceremonial dress and no armour. In addition, the women in the tent had their clothes stripped off. What could be plundered was plundered. Only when ʻUmar Ibn Saʻad came on the scene was there an end to the activity. The Jinns brought the report to Medīna: it was known there before the messenger arrived.

The bodies of the martyrs of Kerbelā' were

buried in Ghādirīya; the heads were cut off and collected. ʿUbaydalla sent them to the Caliph in Damascus; besides Shamir, the noblest Yemenīs had to agree to carry them there: Qays b. Ashʿath al-Kindī, ʿAmr b. Ḥajjāj al-Zubaydī, Azraʿ b. Qays al-Hamdānī (Ṭab.II, p.370). Yazīd was delighted to be able to poke around with his staffs in Ḥusayn's mouth;[22] but he showed himself chivalrous and mild towards the captured women and children. He behaved in a friendly way towards ʿAlī, one of Ḥusayn's sons who was spared in spite of his manhood, and gained his gratitude for it. He allowed the family to return to their home. The leader of the escort was so gentle and compassionate towards the ladies that they gave him their armbands in token of thanks. Their arrival at Medīna aroused loud wailing.

In this account I have based myself upon Abū Mikhnaf. His highly detailed tale is preserved for us almost completely in Ṭabarī, that is in the recension of Ibn Kalbī. The facts added by the latter (from his father, from ʿAwāna, and others) are not essential to the general context. Only in one place does he adopt an essential connecting link from ʿAwāna (Ṭab.II, p.239, l.10). The parallels and the variants which Ṭabarī gives in addition to Abū Mikhnaf do not take up much room. ʿAmmār al-Duhnī agrees with him throughout: he condensed the individual traditions into one short whole and the continuous thread of the story appears clearer in his account.[23] On the other hand, ʿUmar b. Shabba rejects him more strongly, but his varying allegations are not of great value.[24] Neither are those of Ḥusayn b. ʿAbd al-Raḥmān of any greater worth.[25] Apart from Ṭabarī, both Dīnawarī pp.243ss. and Yaʿqūbī II, pp.273ss. should be taken into account although only because of individual notes or verses which they pass on. One must not think that one can learn anything of significance from the committed Shīʿite Yaʿqūbī about an event which was so important for his sect. An independent Shīʿite tradition which goes back to the origins does not exist at all. This only begins at an intermediate point and presupposes the previous existence of an older more unbiassed tradition from which it departs more and more. ʿAmmār al-Duhnī was also a Shīʿite, according to the Fihrist; he agrees on all essential points completely with Abū Mikhnaf. Abū Mikhnaf is the principal authority: he is also recognised as such by the forger who was responsible for the later legends about the death of Ḥusayn being attributed to him.[26]

This specific episode is particularly characteristic of Abū Mikhnaf's style. My extract gives no idea of it. It is all scene and dialogue, although not particularly dramatic. Nothing remains anonymous: every messenger, every servant, every helper who ever said or did anything, even if he only cleaned a sword, is referred to by name. At first sight one cannot see the forest for the trees, so numerous are the details. Thus in the description of Ḥusayn's external appearance one is informed that one of his shoe-laces was torn, and to be exact, the lace of the left shoe.[27] Numerous individual accounts independent of each other were gathered together, often running parallel and bringing the action forward only slowly. Abū Mikhnaf certainly did not assemble them all for the first time; he mentions predecessors and colleagues who had already done this and thus arrived at a certain consensus. (II, p.314, l.7) Yet he is separated by only one generation from those who were contemporary with the event. His chain of authorities for the individual traditions is always quite short, as is the nature of the early, genuine isnād - the later long chain is only a support to preserve appearances, a conventional feature of scriptural authority. The authority from whom he draws his information, had it in his turn directly from an eye witness who took part in the event, or at least he always refers to such people. The eye-witnesses always fall into two groups. Some of them are those who were on Ḥusayn's side, slaves and other escapees,[28] although only a very few of this side escaped, so the majority of the witnesses are those who were on the opposing side. But when relating the story, they no longer adopt the same position. At least as a rule, they regretted their earlier behaviour.[29] Then they sought to play down their share of the guilt, or to bring themselves into favour by the fact that they used the portrayal of their struggle with Ḥusayn in order to glorify him. One may note how lively the debates about the events in Kūfa were and how people constantly excused and blamed each other (Ṭab.II, p.341, pp.344-6).

Abū Mikhnaf collated all the parallel traditions in such a way that the secondary matters retreat into the background because they appear only once and the important matters gradually become prominent because they recur everywhere. The non-parallel ones he places in a suitable series, so that a progressive continuity results from which one cannot depart without picking and choosing. Variants and uncertain traditions do emerge, but there are no essential contradictions on important points. The picture is quite firm and uniform, not only with regard to the facts but also with regard to the characters.

The sole concern of the Ashrāf was to maintain their own position and the narrow interests of their town and their tribes. Although they were fundamentally averse to the Umayyad government, they put their power at its disposal in order to keep peace between the tribes. Indeed, ʿAmr b. Ḥajjāj al-Zubaydī and especially Muḥammad b. Ashʿath al-Kindī acted slavishly to obey the tyrant's orders. In his old age Shabath b. Ribʿī of Tamīm crowned the capacity for change,[30] which he had developed since the days of his youth. After he himself had enticed Ḥusayn to Kūfa, he fought against him. However, the majority of the Kūfans were not intent on playing into the hands of the government, but nor did they go over to the side of its enemies. Even those who wrote letters to Ḥusayn and pledged themselves to him left his emissary in the lurch and raised no hand to help him. At most, they look upon his demise from afar and weep. Only a very few dare go out to share his fate, for example Abū Thumāma the treasurer and Ibn ʿAwsaja. In general, those who suffer death for him are picked up almost by accident on the way or driven to join him at the twelfth hour because of their emotional indignation, although they have nothing to do with him and do not belong at all to his party. The contrast is strongly emphasised and at times dramatically presented[31] between those who neglected their duty and did nothing, and those who had no duty to perform but who put the others to shame. It is noteworthy that not only the Quraysh but also the Anṣār remained aloof from Ḥusayn. None accompanied him from Medīna, and only a very few of them appear amongst the Shīʿites in Kūfa. The revolt in Medīna in the year 63/682 was not undertaken on behalf of the ʿĀlids, and ʿAlī b. Ḥusayn kept apart from it.

In contrast to these cowards and traitors, there are the declared enemies of the Shīʿa, the officials and the supporters of the Umayyad government. The conflict does not revolve around a religious tenet,[32] but around the practical question "Should one be obedient to the government or revolt against it with Ḥusayn?" It is not denied that the 'People of Obedience' considered their behaviour as correct: nonetheless, this is itself condemned and the reason for it not recognised. However the factional tendencies were expressed (in these traditions) more by rhetorical means and easily recognizable biased additions, than by any obscuring or falsifying of the facts. Thus an early tradition as it is presented by Abū Mikhnaf differs from a later one, but very much to its own advantage. Although it also contains diverse fabrications, it provides us with the material from which we can form an independent view about the black sheep. ʿUmar b. Saʿad has qualms of conscience about his action against Ḥusayn. Hence he is viewed with leniency, whilst we find him unpleasant, because he overcame his scruples in order not to let slip the province which he had been promised. Shamir has no scruples, considers the pretender as a disturber of the peace and attacks him decisively. Therefore there exists a prejudice against him which we are not obliged to share. However, in Abū Mikhnaf he is by no means a grotesque rascal or a true heathen full of hatred against the house of the Prophet.[33] He respects, for example, the sanctity of the tent and does not attack Ḥusayn until he has separated him from the tent. ʿUbaydalla is particularly unsympathetic in Abū Mikhnaf's eyes, but yet he presents him to us in a favourable light. Greater praise can scarcely be accorded to him, (i.e. Abū Mikhnaf). The Governor forces his reluctant subjects to serve him; with few means but with clear intent and firm hand, he understands the solution to the difficult problem which was posed for him in unfamiliar, inflamed territory. He did his duty and in no wise exceeded the limits. At most, one can reproach him that he struck Hānī in the face in anger. It was not he but Yazīd who began the crudity with the decapitated head of Ḥusayn. Yazīd is probably too well treated in Tradition.[34] If the killing of Ḥusayn was a crime, then the guilt must be laid on him for he had sent ʿUbaydalla to Kūfa in order to exact severe punishments. Things went well for him and at first he rejoiced over it. If he later became angry with his servant (Ṭab.II, pp.435s.), he was using the master's privilege to blame his own mistakes upon his tools. He certainly cannot be reproached for the calculated friendliness towards the family of Ḥusayn, even if it was only a stratagem which was not heartfelt.

Crucial for the judgement of each personality is their adopted position vis à vis Ḥusayn. He stands in the centre and draws all the interest to himself. Nothing which concerned him is omitted: the minute details lend pathos to his image. He is the theme of numerous speeches, he is preached about and preaches sermons himself with appropriate concluding formulae (Ṭab.II, p.353, l.4): Amen! Amen![35] Miracles, oaths, dreams, prophecies and other religious ingredients adorn the story about him. Anticipating the future, it reports how heaven later punished the murderers of the just man. At all events, the impression of the total futility of the hero remains. Like a clay pot he clashed against the iron ʿUbaydalla. Like the Messiah, he goes along a prepared way to have the kingdom of the world laid at his feet. Like a child he stretches out his hands to the moon. He makes the greatest claims and does not perform the least thing himself. Others must do everything. In fact nobody has any confidence in him. Only those who are in despair drag their hides for him to the market. As soon as he meets opposition, it is all up with him; he wants to go back when it is too late and looks on as his followers die for him in battle, sparing himself until the end. The death of ʿUthmān is a tragedy; that of Ḥusayn a melodrama. But personal defects vanish before the circumstance that the blood of the Prophet flows in his veins, that he belonged to the holy family - Ahl al-Bayt. He did not have to exert himself for he had it all within him. The lack of moral fibre is more than replaced by the apparent physical holiness, as it were, which resides in his flesh and blood. That lends his person its significance,[36] and his history the character of the Islamic passion story. His martyrdom opened a new epoch for the Shīʿa; it meant much more for them than that of his father, who was not the son of the Prophet's daughter. There are certain events which exercise an amazing effect, not because of themselves and their inevitable consequences, but because of their memory in men's hearts.

1. cf. the list in Ṭabarī II, pp.233-235.

2. Also according to Dīnaw, p.254, l.4. Ibn ʿAwsaja in Duhnī's account (Ṭab.II, p.228, l.10) is certainly a mistake.

3. ʿAwāna in Ṭabarī II, p.239, l.10 - p.240, l.5.

4. Disguised according to ʿUmar b. Shabba, Ṭab. p.243.

5. According to Abū Mikhnaf he was furious about that; according to ʿUmar b. Shabba he thereupon took off his dress.

6. This was the title of the officials of the smallest military sections, and civic administrative districts.

7. The statements on this point are doubtful.

8. Ṭab.II, pp.246ss., p.244. (cf. II, p.44, p.53s.) Dīnaw, p.248s.

9. According to ʿUmar b. Shabba (Ṭab.II, p.245) ʿUbaydalla reproached him: "My father on his entry into Kūfa killed all the Shīʿites with the exception of Ḥujr and your father. Now this is how you thank him!" Hānī replied: "I do not wish to forget the favour, you are safe and so is your family!" "What", said ʿUbaydalla's freedman Mihrān, "This daddy-long-legs (i.e. Yemenī) takes you under his protection in the region of your own dominion?" Thereupon he seized him by his two beautifully plaited locks and ʿUbaydalla belaboured his face unmercifully with a staff. The description of Ziyād as the murderer of all Kūfan Shīʿites is sufficient to discredit this report. cf. p.284, ll.8ss.

10. According to the scarcely reliable report of Harūn b. Muslim (Ṭab.II, p.272), prominent amongst them were the well-known Qurayshite Bābba and the even better known Thaqafite Mukhtār.

11. One of them the Qaysite (Fazārite) Asmāʾ b. Khārija was moreover his father-in-law and friendly with the government. cf. The Index

of the Kitāb al-Aghānī. (Guidi)

12. 9th September 780. This is according to Abū Mikhnaf in Ṭab.II, p.271, l.17, (the variant on p.271, l.18 should be corrected according to Mas'ūdī V, p.142), p.272, l.2, p.275, l.20, p.289, l.4. Tuesday is given as the day of the week. 8th Dhū'l-Ḥijja was certainly not a Tuesday, but perhaps the 3rd was, which is given by Dīnawarī, p.256, l.1. However the Tarwiya-day, that is the 8th, seems to remain fixed, at least for the departure of Ḥusayn. Also the week-days do not accord with the later dates of the month of Muḥarram 61 which are certainly correct. Muslim remained in Kūfa about 1½ - 2 months.

13. This contributed to the violent hatred between Zubayrids and 'Ālids, the origins of which lay still further back.

14. He is sometimes confused with the Syrian Ḥusayn b. Numayr, not only by modern historians but also by old Arab scribes. cf. for example Ṭab.II, p.409, l.3 and Dīnaw. p.256, l.4. Qādisiya lay in the path of the approach to Kūfa from the Arabian side.

15. The name is curiously not quoted here by Abū Mikhnaf; cf. Ṭab.II, p.546, l.4, p.1,710, l.8.

16. According to Duhnī (Ṭab.II, p.282), Ḥusayn wanted either to turn back to Medina or to fight on the borders against the heathen, or to be sent to the Caliph. But according to Abū Mikhnaf, (Ṭab.II, p.314), it is incorrect that he made these proposals a matter of choice.

17. For his genealogy, cf. Ṭab.I, p.3,305. Dīnaw. p.267.

18. Allegedly Thursday or Friday; in fact Tuesday.

19. According to Duhnī, Ṭab.II, p.283, he was protected in the rear by reeds.

20. Friday or Saturday are also mentioned.

21. Somewhat greater numbers are quoted by Duhnī, Ṭab.II, p.281 and Ḥusayn p.286. The reference

here is to Ḥusayn b. ʿAbd al-Raḥmān; see p.112, ll.33-4.

22. This is according to Abū Mikhnaf (Ṭab.II, pp.370-383) and Duhnī (Ṭab.II, p.282s.) Ḥusayn cannot compete with this and ascribes this deed to ʿUbaydalla. A staff was usually in the hand of the ruler and it served not only as an insignia (Ṭab.II, p.282, l.18, p.286, l.21, p.523, l.20).

23. Ṭab.II, p.227, ll.16ss., p.281, l.8s. cf. Ṭab.I, p.3,434. cf. The Fihrist, p.220, l.7. (Flügel ed.)

24. Ṭab.II, p.242, ll.10ss., p.273, l.3ss. A comparison of the isnād with that of p.242, ll.10ss. shows that p.272, l.3ss., a fragment with the end missing, is derived also from ʿUmar.

25. Fihrist, p.192. Harūn b. Muslim in Ṭab.II, p.272, ll.3ss., scarcely deserves to be mentioned.

26. cf. Brockelmann, History of Arabic Literature, I, p.65.

27. "I shall never forget that it was the left one" says the eye-witness, p.358, l.8.

28. For example, the servant ʿUqba b. Simʿān and one of the two Asadites who had joined Ḥusayn. Traditions from the members of ʿAlī's family are few and unimportant.

29. In particular Ḥumayd b. Muslim al-Azdī. It is noteworthy that the authorities are mostly not distinguished people. None of the Ashrāf is amongst them.

30. He began his career as verger of the Prophetess Sajāh, accepted Islam when forced, then energetically took the side of ʿAlī against ʿUthmān, was one of the founders of the Khawārij after Ṣiffīn, fought against them at Nahrawān, was along with other heads of the Shīʿa placed under surveillance by Muʿāwiya, and managed to escape from every enterprise upon which he had embarked if it threatened to go wrong.

31. e.g. between Zuhayr b. al-Qayn and ʿAzra b. Qays (Ṭab.II, p.318s.).

32. A certain precedence for the House of the Prophet before all other Arab families is generally recognised (Ṭab.II, p.331, l.8, p.342, l.16, p.350, l.14s.). The title "altglaübig" which A. Müller preferred to use has scarcely any meaning for this period. cf. p.556, l.4, where the Shīʿites call their opponents their religious bretheren.

33. A. Müller I, p.363. At Ṣiffīn, Shamir had fought bravely for ʿAlī and against Muʿāwiya. (Ṭab.I, p.3,305).

34. According to other traditions, Yazīd treated Ḥusayn with respect and regretted the haste with which he had been killed. EI, III, (new edition), p.611. (L)

35. See EI (new edition), I, p.436. (Ed.)

36. The expression Hādī Mahdī is already applied to him, (Ṭab.II, p.350, l.14). Nafs Zakīya is used in a general sense on p.319, l.4. But cf. Agh. VII, p.7, l.26.

CHAPTER 3.

Those Kūfans who had dragged Ḥusayn into the mire and then left him there were conscience-stricken as they saw the results of their actions before their eyes. They felt the need to requite God and to make good their former renunciation through self-sacrifice; they called themselves "the Repenters, the Penitents". Now they made the first attempt at formal organization. Soon after the death of Ḥusayn they formed a society. About one hundred men belonged to it, none of whom was under sixty years old; thus they were not spurred on by passion but by religious conscience. Their Sheikh was the Khuzā'ite Sulaymān b. Ṣurād, also a companion of the Prophet,[1] who earlier had been the leader of the zealous Shī'ites and had taken a prominent part in the summoning of Ḥusayn. In addition to him they had also four other chiefs from the tribes of Fazāra, Azd, Bakr and Bajīla.[2] Every Friday they assembled in Sulaymān's compound and heard him pronounce the self-same words: "Do as the early Israelites, after they had fashioned the golden calf and worshipped it. When Moses said to them, 'You have sinned gravely, now expiate it through death', they meekly stretched out their necks and yielded to the knife, because they recognized that only thus could they be freed of their guilt. Therefore do you likewise; make yourselves ready for death, sharpen your swords and spears and get your war-gear and horses!"

Until Yazīd's death, the movement remained clandestine; only after that did they increase in number and area. Then it was that the Kūfans declared themselves independent of 'Ubaydalla, who was living in Baṣra, and expelled his permanent regent from their city, the Qurayshite 'Amr b. Ḥurayth. The instigators were not the Shī'ites, but the Ashrāf: at their head was Yazīd b. Ruaym al-Shaybāni, who thereby gained great renown. During the interregnum, at first 'Umar b. Sa'ad was made governor designate, then another Qurayshite.

In the meantime, Ibn Zubayr had gained general recognition in Iraq. The Ashrāf of Kūfa also recognized him as Caliph, although they were not attracted to him in all sincerity. (Ṭab.II, p.531). Sent by him, the Anṣārī ʿAbdalla b. Yazīd came as Governor to Kūfa, on Friday 22nd Ramaḍān, 64 (Friday 13th May, 684). (Ṭab.II, p.509).

This upheaval was favourable for the Shīʿites, although they hated Ibn Zubayr, who had established himself as heir to Ḥusayn. They now became bolder and recruited from wider circles. They had the sympathy of the masses with them, even though the Ashrāf wanted nothing to do with them (Ṭab.II, p.531). In their responsible position they were only concerned with averting all disturbance and danger from Kūfa. Amongst the recruiting officers[3] ʿUbaydalla b. ʿAbdalla al-Murrī stood out. He was quite happy to repeat himself constantly and so convince his listeners all the more. "The only way to seek pardon with God is to throw ourselves into battle, even if we perish because of it. The dead are better off than we who are alive and tortured by our guilt." The number of followers increased. About 16,000 men are supposed to have felt it their duty to come forward, not just committed party members. By correspondence also, links were established with Madā'in and Baṣra. Nor did they delay in addition collecting money and weapons.

The watchword was: "Revenge for Ḥusayn!" A practical aim was not firmly established. They were uncertain as to which way one should sell one's life. The next step should have been to subdue the city of Kūfa itself and to drive out the Ashrāf, for they, by their submission to power, now bore the principal guilt for the demise of Ḥusayn, and furthermore were in a state of great anxiety. The majority of the Shīʿites were in favour of that, but Sulaymān was against it, saying that one should not antagonize such influential people. He made them turn against the real enemy and criminals - against the Umayyad government and especially against ʿUbaydalla b. Ziyād, who had gone to Syria, and was then in the field with a large Syrian army, in order to reconquer Mesopotamia as the next step for Marwān. The cunning tolerance of the Kūfan governor ʿAbdalla b. Yazīd contributed much to this decision. The Ashrāf advised him to intervene against the Shīʿites. But he said: "They have only to come out into the open, and I would help them against their enemy, who is also our enemy; that is ʿUbaydalla b. Ziyād, who is only one day's journey distant from the Bridges at Manbij. I consider it more advisable to wage war against him than to arouse civil-war in Kūfa, and so play into his hands." The Shīʿites could now make their preparations against Ibn Ziyād quite openly. They all decided to congregate in the same camp at Nukhayla (near Kūfa) before 1st Rabīʿ II, 65 (15th November 684) and they also summoned their companions from Madāʿin and Baṣra. Their agreement with the governor certainly did not extend, according to his proposal, to their making common cause against the Syrians with him and the Kūfan tribal chiefs.

Of the 16,000 men who had said they would come, only 4,000 appeared on the agreed date at Nukhayla. It was still quite enough for the slaughter. Amongst them were Arabs from all tribes, many Qur'ān readers, but no Mawālī. Although they were in part poor, they were all mounted and well armed. On Friday 5th Rabīʿ II, 65 (Saturday[4] 19th November 684), they marched out towards Kerbelā'. There they stayed for 24 hours at Ḥusayn's grave and confessed their guilt, as they wept and made vows. The crowd at the grave was worse than at the black stone of Mecca.[5] Then they went over the Euphrates, via Haṣṣāṣa, Anbār, Ṣanduda (or Ṣadūd), Qayāra and Hīt towards Qarqīsiyā. Zufar b. Ḥārith who opposed the Umayyad hegemony in Qarqīsiyā at the head of the Qaysites, opened a cheap market for them , gave them information about the movement of ʿUbaydalla, who was now in Raqqa, and advised them to go along the Khaboras up Resayna and to wait for the Syrians there in fortified positions.[6] They followed him and pitched camp to the west of Resayna, protected from behind by the city. They were able to rest there for five days before they were attacked by two of the five Syrian army corps. The battle began on Wednesday 22nd Jumādā I, 65 (Wednesday 4th January, 685), and it lasted until the Friday.[7] The Shīʿites resisted like lions but were finally killed by arrows. The few who escaped had a bad conscience, as though they had failed in their task. They were not pursued in retreat and on the way they met their brothers from Baṣra and Madā'in, who had failed to keep the rendevous at the right time and now came after them when it was too late. They wept together and went on their way.

It was more a feeling of guilt than a duty of
revenge which drove these Shī'ites into battle and
to death.   Had they but shown half the zeal for the
living Ḥusayn which they had for the dead one,
things might have turned out differently.   The
chronicler of the "Repentant Ones" is Abū Miḵẖnaf
and his chief authority is once again Ḥumayd b.
Muslim al-Azdī, who, from being one of Ḥusayn's
murderers, had become one of his enthusiastic supporters;   his witness in poetry is A'shā of Hamdān
(Ṭab.II, p.572ss.).   The speeches take up a great
deal of space.   They were not composed by the
writer, but transmitted.   Once, it is related, the
witness forgot the beginning of a learned speech by
Sulaymān.   Twice it it mentioned that the authority
heard the sermon of a recruiting officer so often,
that he knew it by heart.   The word by word account
is related according to the memory of a man who had
read the original in the time of the Caliph Sulaymān,
and had immediately committed it to memory.

---

1.   But the name Sulaymān contradicts this.

2.   Thus none was a chief of the genuine Yemenīs
     (Hamdān, Maḏẖḥij, Kinda).

3.   These recruiting officers (Dā'ī) are henceforth
     a particularly characteristic feature of the
     Shī'a.

4.   Begins on the evening of the previous day.

5.   This martyr-cult is thus of Arabian, and not
     Persian origin.

6.   The main road from Syria to Iraq goes via
     Manbij or Raqqa over the Euphrates and then via
     Resayna ('Ayn al-Warda) to the Tigris (Ṭab.II,
     p.554, 1.5, p.783, 1.16).   The river route
     goes from Anbār through Nahr al-Malik to Madā'in.

7.   According to Ṭabarī II, p.576, 1.2, the battle
     occurred still in Rabī' II, agreeing with
     Muḵẖtār's remark (p.569, 1.7) that it would
     last for longer than 10 days, but less than a
     month, until Sulaymān was destroyed.   But the
     exact dates of Abū Miḵẖnaf deserve preference,
     because the Shī'ites remembered their martyrs'
     dates properly.

CHAPTER 4.

The defeat of Sulaymān and his followers at Resayna was the beginning of a decisive turn in the inner history of the Shī'ites. The man responsible for that turn in events was Mukhtār b. Abī 'Ubayd, a Thaqafite like Mughīra, Ziyād, 'Ubaydalla and Ḥajjāj, and no less a man than any of these, although a very different type of person.[1] He was of good family - his father led the campaign against the Persians at Buwayb (Nukhayla) and was killed in this unfortunate battle. His brother-in-law was 'Abdalla, the highly distinguished son of the Caliph 'Umar, and his father-in-law was the equally very distinguished Nu'mān b. Bashīr al-Anṣārī. He had a house in Kūfa and an estate in the neighbourhood. His past remains obscure.[2,3] Only after he was sixty years old did he become prominent and it was as a zealous Shī'ite. He came to Kūfa with his Mawālī from his estate Khutarnia, as things were supposed to be starting there after the death of Mu'āwiya. He joined Muslim b. 'Aqīl and participated in the premature revolt of this man.[4] With a black eye, in the truest sense of the word, he escaped the hand of 'Ubaydalla through the intercession of good friends, but he was banished from Kūfa.[5]

He went to the Ḥijāz. On the way he encountered Ibn Irq[6] at Wāqiṣa, and told him that 'Ubaydalla had struck him in the eye, adding: "May God kill me if I do not hack him limb from limb. You shall soon be hearing of me. I shall slay as many men for Ḥusayn as Nebuchadnezzar slew for John the Baptist!" When he saw what an amazing effect his faith made on the other, he added: "Mark my words!" He asked him about Ibn al-Zubayr, and learned that until then he had not come out into the open, but that he would surely do so if he felt strong enough. Thereupon he went to Ibn al-Zubayr and urged him to accept the oath of allegiance in public and offered him his support. But he did this so loudly that Ibn al-Zubayr let him go on his way, angry that his secretive habits were not respected. Mukhtār then disappeared for a longer period from Mecca,[7] until he suddenly re-appeared there and deliberately showed off in the mosque. Now he was better treated by Ibn al-Zubayr. He fought bravely against the Syrians at the beginning of 64/683 in company with the Khawārij of Yamāma.

In Mecca however, he did not find what he expected. After ʿUbaydalla's expulsion from Iraq, he turned his eyes again towards Kūfa. He gathered information about the situation from everyone who came from there. He learned that the Kūfans had given the oath of allegiance to Ibn al-Zubayr but that many of them were inclined to the Shīʿite cause; if only they had the right man at their head they would put him in a position to gobble up the world. Then he cried out: "I am that man! I am the shepherd for the sheep who have no shepherd!" He did not allow himself to be misled by pious warnings about civil war and the Last Judgement; he displayed a remarkable confidence in victory.

Five months and several days after Yazīd's death, he set out on the way to Kūfa. On arriving in the suburbs of Ḥīra, he washed himself and put on ceremonial dress. Accompanied by two Kindites who had joined him, he then rode through the streets of Kūfa into the mosque, everywhere greeting people with the words: "I proclaim to you victory and salvation." It was at the time of the Friday prayer, Friday 15th Ramaḍān, 64 (6th May, 684). After the end of the service, he remained for hours standing by a column in prayer, drawing the eyes of the people upon him.

He planned to make himself the leader of the Shīʿites but did not prosper against Sulaymān b. Ṣurād, despite a certain amount of success. Then Sulaymān was removed from Mukhtār's path by his ill-fated march against the Syrians. Mukhtār was able to take over the inheritance with a good conscience, for he had dissuaded him from this undertaking, the unhappy result of which he foresaw clearly and proclaimed in prophetic speeches. He now took a firm grip on affairs and wanted at first to bring Kūfa itself under his own control and directed the movement of the Shīʿa to this end. The Ashrāf felt threatened and informed the governor ʿAbdalla b.

Yazīd of the behaviour of this dangerous man. He was thereupon arrested, still before the battle of Resayna. To all those who had saved themselves from that defeat, he wrote a letter from prison, which went as follows: "Sulaymān was not the right man, but I am he. I! I! I!" They wanted to set him free from jail but he said that that was unnecessary, as in any case he was soon coming out. On the intercession of his brother-in-law, ʿAbdalla b. ʿUmar, he was indeed released. He made jokes about the oath which he had to swear on pain of dreadful fines, kaffāra, not to revolt against the present Kūfan Government: he would rather pay the fines and give up all his property, than waive his claim to rule. However he did not even have to break his oath for, on Thursday 24th Ramaḍān 65 (14th May 685), a new Governor came to Kūfa to whom he had not sworn the oath. That was the Qurayshite ʿAbdalla b. Muṭīʿ, a zealous follower of Ibn al-Zubayr (Agh.XIII, pp.168ss.).

He was to keep a tighter rein on Kūfa than did his more lenient predecessor. He took the opportunity to proclaim his programme from the pulpit: "I am charged to gather the tribute due to you (the Fay') from the subjects who owe tribute, to pay your pensions from it and to send the excess with your permission to the Caliph in Mecca. So be reasonable and hold your idiots in check. Otherwise you yourselves will have to stand the consequences." But he had touched on a sore point, for the Kūfans without exception were not at all in agreement that the excess of the fay' should be sent away: instead they demanded that it should stay where it was and be shared out. It should be handled according to ʿAlī's example during that period when their city was the seat of the Caliphate and the central treasury, not according to the example of ʿUmar, and least of all according to that of ʿUthmān. Immediately loud opposition was raised in the Mosque by a Shīʿite, who used the occasion to remind them of the popular glory of Kūfa in the time of ʿAlī. Embarassed, the Governor gave way and promised what he could. The man well-aquainted with the situation, the head of the military police, Iyās b. Muḍārit al-ʿIjlī, informed him of the symptomatic significance of the event; the forward person who had cried out in protest belonged to the intimate circle of Mukhtār, and Mukhtār had to be forestalled for he was on the point of acting. Mukhtār was now summoned. But, warned by the messenger, a man of his region, he pleaded sickness and was able to carry on unharmed his preparations to resort to rebellion at the New Year in 66/685. However, things did not progress as quickly as he thought.

One of ʿAlī's sons named Muḥammad lived in Medīna; he was not born of the daughter of the Prophet but of a woman of the tribe of Ḥanīfa,[8] and was called Ibn al-Ḥanafīya after her. Mukhtār appeared in his name and tried to win support for him as the true leader of the Theocracy. He called him the Mahdī, the Messiah. He made himself out to be his trusted regent (Amīn) and agent (Wazīr). Several Shīʿites doubted whether he had done so rightly or not, and went to Medīna to make sure. Ibn al-Ḥanafīya said that he was content to have anyone who would free the ʿĀlids from their enemies through God's agency.[9,10] This evasive reply satisfied those who were easily convinced. After a month, they returned and brought the information to Mukhtār. He felt relieved of weightier care and immediately called a meeting, made a great speech and called down shame upon those who had doubted him.

But he had still to win over another man in Kūfa itself, without whose support the leaders of the Shīʿa promised no success against the Ashrāf and the Governor. He was Ibrāhīm b. Ashtar, the chief of the Nakhaʿ of Madhḥij, an energetic, crafty and independent man. He was truly devoted to ʿAlī's cause, as his father had been, and was also in league with Ibn al-Ḥanafīya, but until then he was not in favour of the specific Shīʿite movement as it had emerged of late. He had not showed himself in favour of Sulaymān b. Ṣurād, nor did he want anything to do with Mukhtār. The attempts to get him to change his mind were not successful. Finally, a letter was brought to him in which Ibn al-Ḥanafīya himself ordered him to recognize Mukhtār. He took offence that the former called himself the Mahdī in it, something he had not done previously; and moreover, that those who brought over the letter, namely Mukhtār himself and some ten others, should claim to represent the legitimacy. Only two attracted his attention by their reserved attitude, the great law and ḥadīth scholar Amīr al-Shaʿbī and his father Shurahīl. He took the Amīr to one side and asked whether he distrusted the witnesses of the legitimacy. "God forbid", replied he. "They are the most distinguished Qur'ān readers, the Shaykhs of the city and the knights of the Arabs!" Thereupon he had him declare the names of all the witnesses and drew up a formal protocol of the procedure. After he had thus saved himself, he complied with the demand of the letter and put himself at Mukhtār's service.[11]

Since then he always attended the evening discussions with Mukhtār. The action was planned for Thursday 14th Rabīʿ I, 66/685. The Government, however, learnt of this, although not the exact date, and from the Monday kept the open places occupied - the market beside the principal mosque was occupied by the police under Iyās, the Sabakha in front of the gates by Tamīmites led by Shabath b. Ribʿī, and the cemeteries of the individual quarters were left under the command of the relevant tribes and their leaders.[12,13] Ibrāhīm took a hundred armed men with him when he made his way to Mukhtār on the Tuesday evening. He scorned the idea of avoiding the police, but instead passed directly via the Market, and when Iyās opposed him, he laid him low. With that the signal for hostilities was given earlier than intended. Ibrāhīm showed the decapitated head of the police-chief to Mukhtār as a sign that no further delay was possible. It was difficult to raise the alarm amongst the party members during the night and to get them through the occupied places. Nevertheless, it passed off without any real battle taking place and Ibrāhīm did the best he could. On the morning of Wednesday, 13th Rabīʿ I (18th October 685) Mukhtār had already arranged his men by the monastery of Hind on the Sabakha, and there he performed the early morning prayer with them. No Imām made such good speeches as he did. He also had many Mawālī (Freedmen) there under his banner, and these men in particular were zealously devoted to him.

The Governor also had given all his men their orders during the night. Shabath was in command on the Sabakha and had Yazīd b. Ruaym with him. He defeated a small party sent against him then turned against Mukhtār himself. At first his troops held back, until he scolded them: "Curses upon you! Do you want to flee before your slaves?" That had the desired effect, he appealed to their honour and turned their rage against the Mawālī who fought for Mukhtār. If one of these was captured, he was immediately slain,[14] whilst Arab prisoners were released. Mukhtār's group, whose cavalry leader was Yazīd b. Anas al-Asadī, were hard pressed in the face of this superiority and, despite desperate resistance, would certainly have been defeated had Ibrāhīm finally not intervened. He had in the meantime dispersed the two assembled enemy corps in the city against which he had been detached and now was able to hurry to the help of Mukhtār. As soon as he appeared, Shabath's troops vacated the field and fled. In the city they assembled once again with the remainder, mainly on the Kunāsa, but were driven away from there also by the all-powerful Ibrāhīm. The Ashrāf and the Governor, Ibn Muṭī', now fled into the citadel and were besieged there. The number of Shī'ites increased greatly after the victory! After three days Ibn Muṭī' slipped out and hid himself, the Ashrāf surrendered, and recognized Mukhtār. On the next morning, he received the oath of allegiance in the citadel "on the basis of the Word of God, the Sunna of the Prophet, revenge for the blood of the holy family, the war against the unfaithful and the sheltering of the weak". With the nine million which he found in the Treasury, he rewarded his warriors. The first 3,800 men, who had borne the burden and heat of the day, got 500 dirhems; the 6,000 who had only turned up after the victory and had helped besiege the citadel got 200 each.

Without much bloodshed Mukhtār had won control over Kūfa. He made efforts to act lawfully and leniently, to calm people's minds and appease the factions. At first he ruled the courts himself with great zeal and skill, until it became too much for him and he had to appoint Qāḍīs.[15] He allowed Ibn Muṭī' to go in peace and gave him a handsome gift of money for the journey. Although his battle-cry was "Revenge for Ḥusayn", he restrained his followers from murder and ferocity.[16] Also he pardoned a personal enemy who had treated him badly, and was quite happy to be thanked in verse.

He not only gave the promise of safety to the Ashrāf, but also desired that they occupy under him the same positions as partners and advisers, as they had with his predecessors. To the born representatives of the Kūfan interest, it was quite a welcome thought that he was striving to make the city the capital of the Theocracy again. He chose officials and officers exclusively from the ruling class of the Arab military nobility. But besides this, concern for "the weak" was an important part of his programme. In his eyes this innocuous title taken from spiritual language represented the non-Arab Muslims, the Mawālī. They made up more than half of the inhabitants of Kūfa and had control of artisanship, commerce and business. The Arab soldiers left the provisioning of the city to them.[17] They were in speech and origin mainly Iranians,[18] brought to Kūfa as prisoners of war and there converted to Islam. Then freed by their masters, they were adopted as clients in the Arab tribes, so that they now occupied an intermediate position. They were certainly no longer slaves, but they were still very dependent on their master, in need of his protection and had a duty to serve him. They formed his retinue in times of peace and war. Amongst these Mawālī who were entitled to more than ruling Arabism was willing to grant them, thanks to Islam there now arose the hope that they would be free of their clientship and come to play a full and direct part in the Muslim state. Mukhtār aroused this hope in them, he attracted them and, through them, increased his own Mawālī. He had the greatest trust in them and maintained the closest relations.[19] He chose his body-guard from them and gave command over them to one of their own number. Otherwise, at first he placed only Arabs in the leading positions: originally they too formed by far the majority of the Shī'ite armies and constituted the cavalry. The Mawālī were mostly not mounted and, as a rule, had no swords but used wooden clubs as weapons.[20,21] In the first revolt their numbers did not represent more than 500, and only afterwards did they increase rapidly. But the Arabs on the enemy side who supported the Ashrāf had an interest in describing matters as though from the first they would have had to fight against their slaves, who, not contented with their freedom, now stretched their hands towards the revenues of the state and the resulting pensions.[22] They found it unheard of that the Mawālī should fight for themselves and not, as previously, for their masters. Their hatred made them cunning and from the beginning enabled them to recognize the distinctive feature of the now emergent Shī'ite movement, which at first was not so clearly defined. In this way they certainly were responsible for talking of the Devil and making him appear, and exacerbated the opposition between

Arabs and Mawālī. Mukhtār did not manage to bridge these differences. He did not win over the Arab national party and also ran the danger of upsetting the Mawālī. He had prevented them from taking revenge on Ḥusayn's murderers, that is on the Ashrāf. The Mawālī grumbled about his flattering them, about his wavering between both sides. Abū Amra Kaysān, the chief of the body-guard brought this knowledge to his ears. He had to pacify them and did so by making secret declarations which they could interpret as they wished. It does not follow in any way that he was not serious about his policy of appeasement, with the aim to unite the Arabs and the Mawālī through Islam. He did not abandon this deliberately, but was forced by circumstances. He was obliged to set up a party government made up of those whom he could trust most and who ran to him in the greatest number after the victory.

At first external events established his position. The new officials whom he sent to the provinces dependent on Kūfa, were accepted without opposition. Only the pious rebel ʿUbaydalla b. Ḥurr, who had established himself in Madā'in and the territory of Jūkhā, refused to obey him. On the other hand, a revolt of the Baṣran Shīʿites misfired in his favour.[23] In spite of all the hostility which he had incurred by opposing his rule in Iraq, Mukhtār thought that he could avoid an open breach with Ibn Zubayr - even after he had prevented by force of arms the entry into Kūfa of the new Governor with whom Ibn al-Zubayr had wished to supplant the expelled Ibn Muṭīʿ. He offered him aid against the common enemy, the Syrians, who in 66/685 had pressed into Arabia as far as Wādī'l-Qūrā and obtained permission that he, Mukhtār, should send an army of 3,000 Mawālī to Medīna led by Shurahbil b. Wars al-Hamdānī. They were supposed to operate together with 2,000 of Ibn al-Zubayr's warriors who marched from Mecca against the Syrians led by ʿAyyāsh b. Sahl al-Anṣārī.[24] But ʿAyyāsh eliminated these embarrassing allies by means of cowardly murder - they were of course only Mawālī - doubtless on the orders of his chief, whose evil deeds and perfidy knew no bounds. Now Mukhtār of necessity lowered his mask and showed himself clearly opposed to Ibn Zubayr. To this end, he refreshed his somewhat one-sided relationship with Ibn Ḥanafīya and offered to send him troops to Medīna (against Ibn al-Zubayr) if he would publicly declare himself in his favour. But he got a negative answer, which he understandably kept to himself. However, Ibn Ḥanafīya was soon confronted with the situation of having to accept his support, and even to ask for it, because when he had gone for the Ḥajj of 66/685 to Mecca,[25] he and his supporters were surrounded by Ibn al-Zubayr within the shrine and threatened with death if he did not perform the oath of allegiance within an agreed space of time. Thereupon he turned to Mukhtār. He succeeded in sending a letter to him describing his distress and imploring his help. Greatly gladdened, Mukhtār read out the letter in public and immediately had volunteer troops go to Mecca.[26] The first 150 were sufficient to free Ibn al-Ḥanafīya but he refused them the permission which they demanded to take revenge upon Ibn al-Zubayr. Ibn al-Zubayr had at first spoken brave words but now made very little noise as masses of club-carrying men poured one after another into Mecca. All in all they amounted to 4,000 men. Ibn al-Ḥanafīya shared out amongst them the money which they had brought him and they withdrew with it.

The opportunity which Mukhtār had sought in Arabia to fight against the Syrians, he found in Mesopotamia without seeking! Towards the end of the year 66/685, after a long wait they finally turned back again towards the Tigris, under the command of ʿUbaydalla b. Ziyād. Mukhtār despatched 3,000 cavalry[27] against them led by Yazīd b. Anas al-Asadī. At day break on the 9th Dhū'l-Ḥijja, 66 (7th July 686), in the neighbourhood of Moṣul, they met with a force of Syrian troops double their number. They defeated them after two days of skirmishing. Yazīd b. Anas went away sick, being near to death as he directed the battle. He had to be supported on both sides of the donkey on which he sat and, in the evening after the victory, he died. Thereupon the other leaders decided to retreat, for they dared not make contact with the approaching main Syrian force, estimated at 80,000 men.

In Kūfa the rumour spread that the Shīʿites had been defeated by the Syrians. Mukhtār quickly ordered Ibrāhīm b. Ashtar with 7,000 men to the battle area. In these circumstances, the courage of the Ashrāf, the leaders of the Arab national party, grew stonger against him. They accused him of the following: "He has claimed the ruler's position on his own authority, without authorization from Ibn al-Ḥanafīya. He and his party (through a new sort of Islam) have renounced our pious ancestors; he has enticed our slaves and Mawālī, and mounted them, has given or promised them a share of our state revenue: in this way he has robbed us, for we have given them freedom in the hope of a reward from God and thanks from them. Thus he has impoverished our orphans and widows."[28] The principal spokesman in these speeches was the old Shabath b. Ribʿī of Tamīm. He went to Mukhtār in order to present the complaints to him. Mukhtār promised them to consider them as best he could, but asked at the same time: "Will you then fight with me against ʿAbd al-Malik and Ibn al-Zubayr in place of the Mawālī and give me a pledge to that end?" The Ashrāf would not agree to that. They determined rather to take advantage of the favourable situation to overthrow the dictator, although in so doing they betrayed Iraq to the Syrians. Only one of them, the cautious ʿAbd al-Raḥmān b. Mikhnaf, a relative of the narrator Abū Mikhnaf, did not believe in the venture and stressed that Mukhtār not only had the servants and Mawālī on his side, but also the bravest and most capable cavalrymen of the Arabs, and that they were all of one mind and intent: "He will fight against you with the warlike courage of the Arabs and the hatred of the Persians (the Mawālī); leave it to the Syrians and Baṣrans to fight with these people, and avoid any bloody discord in your city!" But because he could not shift the others from their purpose, he made common cause with them. After Ibrāhīm's departure they now occupied the most important areas, restricted Mukhtār to the citadel and the Mosque and severed his communications. In order to delay them, Mukhtār proposed that Ibn al-Ḥanafīya himself be questioned by a delegation about him and his legitimacy, but in vain.

But he found ways and means to inform Ibrāhīm and to send him the order to return with all speed. The messenger needed only a day to get to Sabat on the Tigris where he overtook Ibrāhīm, and on the evening of the next day, Ibrāhīm with his troops reached Kūfa and camped with them beside the Mosque during the night.

On the next morning, Wednesday 24th Dhū'l-Ḥijja, 66,[29] there ensued a repeat of the battles of the month of Rabīʿ. The opposing positions overlapped strangely within the two factions, as far as the Arabs on all sides were concerned. Many of the Arab Shīʿites, who until then had supported Mukhtār's side, now defected and supported the Ashrāf. In particular there was the prominent Qur'ān reader, Rifāʿa b. Shaddād al-Fityānī, an old friend of Sulaymān b. Ṣurād. But he was sadly disappointed as, when in answer to the Shīʿite war-cry "Yā latharāt Ḥusayn", there came the reply "Yā latharāt ʿUthmān"[30] on the side of the Ashrāf and he committed suicide in despair. In addition ʿAbdalla b. Qurād al-Khathʿamī had great qualms about shedding the blood of his own family, but he remained loyal to Mukhtār. On the other hand, the son of Shabath b. Ribʿī fought decisively for Mukhtār against his own father. The Ashrāf had taken up position with their tribes on three open places: the Muḍar stood on Kunāsa, the Yemenīs on the Jabbānat Sabīʿ (which adjoined the Sabakha) and the Rabīʿa were outside on the Sabakha itself. The hottest battle raged on the Jabbānat Sabīʿ, where Mukhtār in person opposed the Yemenīs, that is essentially the Hamdānids, because the Madhḥij (to whom Ibrāhīm belonged) stayed aside from the fighting. The decisive moment occurred when the Shibām of Hamdān maliciously fell upon their own tribe in the rear. Thus fanaticism destroyed respect for blood ties: "O marvel! Mukhtār, who himself has no people, attacks me with my own people!" With the defeat of the Hamdān, of whom 780 men were killed, things were concluded. The Muḍar were easily routed by Ibrāhīm (who did not wish to fight against the Yemenīs) and the Rabīʿa dispersed themselves without having drawn their swords at all. The Yemenīs were particularly active on both sides, as much on the national-Arab side, as on the Shīʿite, for they were the most numerous and strongest group in Kūfa.

After the victory, Mukhtār proclaimed that all those who went home and locked the door behind them would be safe. But he deliberately made an exception of the murderers of Ḥusayn from this safe-conduct and gave free rein to the revenge-seeking Shīʿites, whom until then he had restrained within limits. After the first of the prisoners had been executed, there followed others: the guilty ones of Kerbelā' were gradually dragged out of their hiding places, supposedly on the order of the puppet in Medīna, Ibn Ḥanafīya. The slaves and the Mawālī were like blood-hounds on the heels of their former masters; wives betrayed their husbands. Not only Shamir b. Dhī Jawshān, but also ʻUmar b. Saʻad and numerous other Qurayshites had to die. Whoever of the Ashrāf was able, fled to Baṣra to Muṣʻab.[31] Their houses in Kūfa were destroyed, but their families which remained behind were protected by Mukhtār (Ṭab.II, p.719). He himself was not as a rule the worst offender; many were murdered without his knowledge and against his orders. However, he spared Surāqa b. Mirdās al-Bāriqī only because he was a poet who had written verses saying that Mukhtār's enemies had seen the angels fighting on his side, and that they were put to flight by the angels. Mukhtār forced him to deny his poetic lies publicly from the pulpit and to swear an oath, and then he banished him from Kūfa.

Two days after quashing the revolt, Mukhtār sent Ibrāhīm back against the Syrians, with the order to attack them as soon as he found them. He himself accompanied the troops advancing to battle as far as the Euphrates, and gave them promises of victory on the difficult journey. The battle with the Syrians took place by the river Khazir, which flows through the Great Zāb into the Tigris. Surprisingly, the date is not given anywhere but it certainly falls in the first month of the year 67 (August 686).[32] The Shīʻites defeated forces ten times stronger than themselves, as a result of the skill of their leader and their own bravery. The white doves were not allowed to fly,[33] and the treachery of the Qaysites in the Syrian army, if it really took place, only ensued after the decisive moment (Ṭab.II, p.712s.). ʻUbaydalla b. Ziyād was slain; Ḥusayn b. Numayr and Shurahbil b. Dhilkulaʻ were also killed in revenge for the holy cities, for Ḥusayn, and for Mālik al-Ashtar. The fleeing Syrians for the most part drowned in the water, their camp was plundered. Whilst the first group of Mukhtār's conscripts, led by Yazīd b. Anas, was completely mounted, the second had almost no cavalry at all (Ṭab.II, p.709, 1.5, p.721, 11.11ss.), that is, it consisted of Mawālī. They beat with their clubs on the helmets and shields of the enemy to such an extent that it rang like the beating noises in the factory of Walīd b. ʻUqba b. Abī Muʻayṭ - so goes the account of an early authority. Arab tradition is ashamed to quote the names of these heroes. Ibrāhīm remained on the watch for the

Syrians in Mosul, while his step-brother conquered Nisibis,[34] Dārā and Sinjār.

Mukhtār stood on the heights and in front of him lay the abyss. The Arab Shī'ites of long standing distrusted him and many defected. Thus he found himself obliged to rely upon the fanatics and the Mawālī, and was forced completly on to their side against the national-Arab faction. He impressed them with his self-assurance and the ceremonial manner by which he proclaimed himself.[35] We are told of an agitated scene which took place when he accompanied Ibrāhīm to the Euphrates. There the extreme Shī'ites crowded the bridge which he wished to cross so that he had to choose another way. They had a holy chair with them carried by a mule and tended by one special priest. They danced and jumped around it in frantic manner as they prayed for victory, in understandable excitement at the departure and the enormous danger into which they were going. This was anathema to sober-minded people. Mukhtār himself was probably innocent of the nonsense but he did not wish to ruin the people's pleasure. He could not dispense with their help for they would go through fire for him.

The Syrians were defeated and crippled for years to come. Danger now threatened from Baṣra where, since the end of 66/685 or the beginning of 67/686,[36] Muṣ'ab b. Zubayr had governed under the command of the Meccan Caliph, his elder brother. He was urged to act against Mukhtār by the Kūfan Ashrāf who had fled, particularly by the Tamīmite Shabath b. Rib'ī and by the Kindite Muḥammad b. Ash'ath. The Baṣran troops were then in the field against the Khawārij and their leader Muhallab was not altogether prepared to leave the Khawārij in order to fight against the Mawālī of Kūfa. However, he eventually allowed himself to be persuaded and took the command of the great army which, before the middle of 67/686, marched out from Baṣra. One of 'Alī's sons, 'Ubaydalla, also took part in the expedition. Mukhtār sent his men to Madhār[37] on the Tigris. There they were to wait for the enemy; on the basis of an old oracular promise, they would be victorious there. But they suffered a dreadful defeat. The victors gave no quarter; the Kūfans who had fled to Baṣra raged mercilessly against their countrymen. Their swords made particularly terrible inroads into the Mawālī. They fought in the bravest manner but were shamelessly left in the lurch by their Arab comrades, the Bajīla and the Khath'am. They could not flee because they had no horses. Only a few mounted men escaped.

This defeat made a deep impression in Kūfa. Mukhtār's prestige sagged. This time he had lied, said the Mawālī. He himself remarked drily: "The slaves had to bite the dust". He was composed and resolved. He let out the waters of the Euphrates near Saylahin,[38] into the four canals which started from there, hoping to beach the ships containing the enemy infantry, but their cavalry repaired the damage and floated the ships off again. Muhallab pressed forward from Anbār towards Kūfa and, at Ḥarūrā', he came upon Mukhtār and his men. An even fiercer battle raged; Muḥammad b. Ash'ath, the leader of the Kūfans in the Baṣran army, was killed with his companions; 'Ubaydalla b. 'Alī also fell under the sword-blows of those who idolized his family. Muhallab held back his Azdites and Tamīmites in reserve and did not turn towards Muṣ'ab who wished to engage him. Only when the time appeared ripe did he bring them into the battle and their attack decided it. The bodies of the noblest Shī'ites of Kūfa covered the field. Mukhtār fought on foot the whole night through, until he was almost alone. Then he followed the few who held out with him and withdrew into the citadel.[39]

Ibrāhīm b. Ashtar had remained in Moṣul although he hardly needed to do so because of the Syrians. Mukhtār must have had his reasons not to call him; he did not consider him a trust-worthy companion. Had he been present, things might easily have followed a different course. The Shī'ite soldiers were at least a match for the Baṣrans; they only lacked a leader. Ibrāhīm might well have taken up with Muhallab, bu instead he now made peace with Muṣ'ab and remained true to him until death.

On the morning after the battle, the Baṣrans reached the outskirts of Kūfa (through the main access from the Sabakha) and then closed the net around Mukhtār tighter and tighter and cut off his supplies.[40] He held the citadel and the inner city. There were about a thousand Mawālī and only about a hundred Arabs with him, the majority of the Arabs having slipped away to their families. Women brought him water. But fear of him began to dwindle; sometimes he was sprinkled with filthy water as he passed through the alleys. He found himself finally confined to the Citadel, without water and food. After the siege, that is the street fighting, had lasted four months long,[41] he ordered his men to make an attempt to break through. In vain. They refused, saying that they preferred to surrender unconditionally. Then he alone made a sortie with 19 men and was killed on 14th Ramaḍān 67 (3rd April 687). He was then 67 years old.

All those who surrendered their arms were executed. Their number reached from six to eight thousand. Muṣʻab gave in to the Kūfan aristocrats' rage, who wished to avenge the blood of their fathers and relatives on the Mawālī. Thus he gained the nickname of "The Butcher". In Ibn ʻUmar someone says to him: "If you had killed only 7,000 sheep from the herd of your father, even then it would have been too many." He aroused the deepest indignation by executing Mukhtār's wife, a daughter of Nuʻmān b. Bashīr al-Anṣārī, who still would not renounce her husband's prophethood. The hand of the Arab Knipperdolling[42] was nailed to the mosque.[43]

Ṭabarī here again reproduces almost exclusively the account of Abū Mikhnaf.[44] He tells his story in this case mainly through one intermediary authority, but sometimes even from eye-witnesses. Amongst them, and of interest, are Ḥumaid b. Muslim al-Azdī (Ṭab.II, p.536s. p.659), to whom we have already referred frequently, then al-Shaʻbī (p.609ss. p.684, p.715s.) and ʻAbd al-Raḥmān b. ʻUbaid Abī 'l-Kunūd (p.663, l.10); they were all three at first on Mukhtār's side and afterwards defected. In general almost all the primary authorities were disloyal and turn-coats. There are no Mawālī amongst them, with one exception (p.621, l.10). The story is told from the Arab point of view. The Mawālī are an obscure, anonymous mass, whilst the names of Arabs abound. The account remains more sympathetic to the Shīʼites, than against them. The sufferings which they had to undergo were, however, (p.624, l.13ss.) greatly exaggerated in a provocative speech made by one of their leaders. In general, Abū Mikhnaf's account of the facts does not seem to have suffered from prejudice. He is extremely accurate, partly in the chronological and always in the topographical details, a fuller understanding of which would certainly require a map of old Kūfa. The remarks of the Mawālī were sometimes authentically reproduced, that is in Persian, just as some words of Christ occur in Aramaic in Mark's Gospel. Of the poets, one finds quotes from ʿAbdalla b. Ḥammām (Ṭab.II, p.636ss. p.640ss.), Surāqa b. Mirdas (p.664s. p.716), Miskīn b. ʿĀmir (p.685s.), Mutawakkil al-Laythī (p.686, p.705), ʿUmar b. Abī Rabīʿa (p.744), Saʿīd b. ʿAbd al-Raḥmān b. Ḥassān b. Thābit (p.745s.), ʿUqba al-Asadī (p.750) and especially Aʿshā Hamdān (p.670, p.674, p.704s., p.723, pp.729ss.).

---

1. Van Gelder deals with him in a detailed and highly noteworthy dissertation, Leiden 1888 (Brill).

2. According to Ṭab.II, p.14 (p.520, l.14), he advised his uncle, who commanded Madā'in, to seize Ḥasan and to hand him over to Muʿāwiya. Contrary to this he avoided putting his name to the accusation against Ḥujr, according to II, p.134, l.4, at the request of Ziyād. The account of Ṭab.II, pp.740-748 merits no refutation.

3. Mukhtār was in the service of ʿAlī. See C. Cahen, "Points de Vue sur la Révolution ʿabbāside", Revue Historique, 230 (1963), p.303. (L)

4. Ṭab.II, p.272, pp.520ss.

5. Ṭab.II, p.522. cf.II, p.536s., p.600.

6. The man is supposed to be well-known, but I can find out nothing about him.

7. In the meantime, he gave a guest performance in the city of Ṭā'if, Ṭab.II (p.526, l.8). Van Gelder (p.29) suspects that he then established relations with Ibn Ḥanafīya in Medīna.

8. She was called Khawla (Agh. VII, p.4). Another Khawla, of Fazāra, had married Ḥasan b. ʿAlī (Agh. XI, p.36).

9. The suspicion of Van Gelder quoted on p.134, note 1, is thus scarcely probable.

10. Muhammad b. al-Ḥanafīya probably accepted Mukhtār's offer of support but it is doubtful that he was titled Mahdī. This is a later concept. Cahen, Révolution ʻabbāside, pp.304-5; W.M. Watt, "Shīʻism Under the Umayyads", Journal of the Royal Asiatic Society, 1960, p.162. (L)

11. Thus the Amīr al-Shaʻbī (that is of the family of Shaʻbān of Hamdān) himself relates, according to Abū Mikhnaf.

12. The Sabakha, a large desert plain, lay in front of the city in the direction of the Euphrates. The market beside the principal Mosque extended into the Kunāsa (Place of Grief). In addition there were smaller squares in the individual quarters. They are called in Persian Chahārsūj(Four-cornered, square. Ṭab.II, p.733, l.11) and in Arabic Jabbāna and are named after the families which lived in the neighbourhood. They were probably situated near the tribal Mosques (which are comparable to the chapels beside a Cathedral) and correspond to our cemetries. They originally served as burial places but later for all possible purposes for which the narrow winding streets were not suitable.

13. A full account of the topography of Kūfa and the distribution of Arab tribes in the city may be found in L. Massignon, "Explication du plan de Kūfa", Mémoires de l'Institut Français d'Archéologie Orientale, Cairo, LXVII, pp.337-360. (L)

14. "Thou son of a harlot. Thou hast left thy fish-trade lying on the Kunāsa, and hast taken up arms to thank him who freed thee by killing him." This was said to one of them.

15. It is of general interest that the Qāḍī is only the representative of the ruler - in partem curae advocatus.

16. The results of the condensing of the historical material (in Weil) are indicated by A. Müller,

I, p.380: "Mukhtār had nothing more pressing to do than to seize the murderers of Ḥusayn and to have them killed." This is the exact opposite of the truth.

17. They were also workers on the estates near Kūfa, for example on that of Mukhtār who brought them with him from there. There they allowed themselves to mingle with Aramaic Fellāḥīn. ʿAbdalla b. Zabīr called them in verses (Agh. XIII, p.37, l.27) "The Magi of the Villages, and the Jews of the Villages." But the scornful impression should not be emphasised. The Arab soldiers were concentrated in the cities (Kūfa and Baṣra). The non-Arabs do not belong there. "Jew" is a pejorative title. The division between servants and Mawālī is fluid. The Mawālī themselves were called servants, yet they also could have real slaves attached to them. Mukhtār's concern was not for the nationality but for the social standing of the Mawālī: to act for the Persians as such never occurred to him in the least. Yet it was of great significance in the future that the Mawālī were mostly Persians.

18. Iranian soldiers who were captured in war or who surrendered to the Arabs were made mawālī and brought to serve in the Arab armies. Many other mawālī, however, were Aramaeans and Christians from the surrounding countrysides. Watt, Shī'ism, pp.162-65. (L)

19. That was not an exception but the rule amongst the Arab notables.

20. Aʿshā Hamdān said to the Baṣrans who bragged about Mukhtār's defeat, that their merit was not great since they had had to deal with unarmed people. (Ṭab.II, p.684, l.11). Because of their clubs, the Mawālī were called the "cudgel-men" (Ṭab.II, p.684, l.16, p.693, l.4, p.1,798, l.4s., p.1,804, l.12. Agh. V, p.155, VIII, p.33, XI, p.47, XIII, pp.166ss.) Their weapon is called "heretic-hammer" (Ṭab. II, p.694, l.15) which now is as a rule used only for that of the followers of Abū Muslim.

21. In arabic they were sometimes called Awlād al-Khashabīya. (Ed.)

22. Tab.II, p.631.

23. Letter of Mukhtār to Aḥnaf. Ṭab.II, p.685.

24. Against Ṭab.II, p.689, l.12, cf. II, p.579, l.1.

25. This is the only possible opportunity, which is, however, not mentioned by tradition.

26. They were Mawālī; however Arabs were named as the commanders, namely in Ṭab.II, p.694, Agh. VIII, p.32s. Abū ʻAbdalla al-Judalī (of Judayl Azd p.656, l.11), Agh. XIII, p.167s. Abū Ṭufayl ʻĀmir b. Wāthila al-Laythī (Ṭab.II, p.1,054, p.1,067). The Meccan expedition took place perhaps only at the beginning of 67/686, after the battle at Khāzir. cf. Wāqidī in Ṭab.II, p.748.

27. One would think the cavalry was comprised of Arabs. But there were also Mawālī amongst them. (Ṭab.II, p.647, l.6).

28. These women needed the servants most of all and had at the same time least power to keep them in check.

29. Ṭab.II, p.667, l.7. But the quoted day of the month (22nd July, 686) fell upon a Sunday.

30. "Oh revenge for Ḥusayn! Oh Revenge for ʻUthmān." (Ed.)

31. Asmā b. Khārija al-Fazārī, the father-in-law of ʻUbaydalla b. Ziyād fled to Syria. See Agh. XIII, pp.36ss. (p.37, l.21, read ʻabīduhā for ʻatīduhā).

32. The revolt in Kūfa was, according to Ṭabarī II, p.667, put down on 24th Dhū'l-Ḥijja 66; according to Ṭabarī II, p.701, l.1, Ibrāhīm marched off again two days afterwards, that is on the 26 of that month, so he could not have reached the region of Mosul before the new year. According to Ṭabarī II, p.701, l.3, he certainly marched off again already on 22nd Dhū'l-Ḥijja 66. But the events in Kūfa which begin only a few days after the battle at Mosul on 9 Dhū'l-Ḥijja would then follow each other even more quickly than is anyhow the case.

33. This fairy-tale is found in The Kāmil, pp.598ss. Perhaps the doves originate from the previously mentioned angels which Surāqa had flying for Mukhtār.

34. The "cudgel-people" remained in Nisibis (under Abū Qārib) for a long while after. cf. Agh.V, p.155.

35. Soon after Ibrāhīm had marched away, Mukhtār set off on the way to meet him. In Sabat he predicted through an oracle: "We have triumphed at Nisibis and the enemy is surrounded in Nisibis." In Madā'in the first messengers bringing news of the victory met him and he proclaimed in triumph from the pulpit: "Have I not told it to you!" "Do you still not believe that he has knowledge of the Unseen?" Sha'bī was asked. "Not on this proof", replied he, "for he foretold the victory at Nisibis, whilst the battle was fought on the Khazir". The questioner did not wish for so precise an answer.

36. cf. Ṭab.II, p.688, l.17 (Also II, p.665, l.7, p.716, l.15) against p.717, l.1.

37. The military route from Baṣra to Kūfa did not go through the deserts on the Arabian side of the Euphrates, but over the canals to the Tigris near Madā'in and from there again over the canals to the Euphrates near Anbār. The troops went by ship, the cavalry rode alongside. For the oracular decree, cf. Wāqidī in Ṭab.II, p.748.

38. For the locality, cf. Ṭab.II, p.921, l.8.

39. The date of the battle is not given, for one cannot begin to consider Agh. XIII, p.38, l.1, cf. p.167, l.16 (giving the year as 70/689), l.26. But it emerges from that that Mukhtār's death (on 14th Ramaḍān 67) occurred four months later, and thus falls in the middle of Jumādā I, 67 (beginning December 686). The fact that the moon shone corroborates it. According to Wāqidī in Ṭabarī II, p.748s., the battle began as the moon rose, the Baṣrans were forced back into their camp, but there they applied themselves to their arms bravely; the

followers of Mukhtār defected one after the other, and in the morning he found himself alone.

40. The city was open, only the citadel was fortified. But the narrow inner streets were easily defended.

41. Wāqidī, in Ṭab.II, p.749.

42. Bernhard Knipperdolling: A member of the evangelical movement, later becoming an anabaptist. 1534 became Bürgermeister of Münster. Was beheaded in 1536. (Ed.)

43. His heirs lived still later in Kūfa. Ṭab.III, p.468, l.5. Bal. p.308, p.366.

44. In addition to Madā'inī II, p.680, l.12, p.717, l.3, l.17, p.749, l.17, Wāqidī, II, p.748, l.3, and others, p.651, l.20, p.665, l.13, p.684, l.4, p.702, l.17, p.714, l.2, p.731, l.4, p.746, l.17.

CHAPTER 5.

Mukhtār is called the Magician (Ṭab.II, p.730, l.13), the Antichrist (p.686, l.7s.) and usually the Liar. This judgement is not affected by the fact that he claimed to act on behalf of Ibn al-Ḥanafīya, but more because he emerged as though he were a prophet. He certainly did not describe himself as such, but he did his utmost to create this impression. He spoke as one who was a member of God's council and knew the future, and he preferred to use the form of the old soothsayers, the Saj' style, in which he was a virtuoso. He wanted to impress through his own personality. Indeed he succeeded in this, although less with distinguished and learned people than with the poor folk. As long as he remained successful, he found credence in wide circles. Then came the defeat, which made him an outlaw. Tradition condemned him in retrospect, but originally it only condemned him without deforming his image. That only happened at a rather later stage, the result of certain characteristics which were invented by hatred. It is precisely these characteristics which now determine posterity's portrayal of him. Dozy relies only on them for the characteristics of Mukhtār which he sketches in the Essai sur l'histoire de l'Islamisme, p.223ss: he caused the doves to fly, he became a Khārijite, Zubayrite and Shī'ite one after the other and, in order to justify this fickleness, he had invented the doctrine of the changing habits of God.[1] It is not necessary to make him look ridiculous in order to understand him. Fortunately the publication of Ṭabarī has put an end to this tendency.

If the question whether Mukhtār was a true or a false prophet is to be answered at all, it must be phrased: was he sincere or not? One can reproach him that he used prophethood as a means to the end of attaining the ruling position. Yet this reproach could also be applied to Muḥammad and one must bear in mind that Islam was a political religion and that an Islamic prophet had to strive for the ruling position. Perhaps it weighed more heavily in the balance against him that he concealed himself behind a puppet who knew nothing about him and neither wished to do so. He did not have a good conscience about this; but as things were, it was impossible for him as a Muslim and a Shīʻite to act under his own name. He had to create for himself the position of a general plenipotentiary (Amīn) of the Mahdī, who remained in the background, and thereby created a model for the future. Such daemonic temperaments are always problematical; complete transparency would hardly be praiseworthy for them. The question of his sincerity can only be answered by asking whether he believed in himself or not and, originally, that appears in fact to have been the case. He was in his old age when the higher conviction suddenly awoke. In his case egoism co-existed with a most firm religious faith. When he was still a trivial personality and exposing himself to great danger, he startled the world with his triumphant self-assurance and by the quite open exposition of his aims. It can scarcely be accepted that that was then mere play-acting. He believed in himself much more and in this way found belief amongst others and was able to move the masses. Subsequently, he certainly blew on the ashes in order to keep the fire going. He had had a firm grasp on his purpose, and now himself acted as though carried beyond his will by his blind followers, whose fanaticism he needed and could not dispense with even if he tried. But the beginning is always crucial, for enthusiasm never remains pure and Mutanabbī emerges quite easily from Nabī.[2] It is, however, sheer slander to say that in the last resort he cynically recognized his own hypocrisy, and scorned his loyal followers. That is sufficiently contradicted by the fact that his wife, a noble Arab woman from Medīna, suffered martyrdom for him after his death, because she refused to deny her faith in him. There were also others who maintained their attachment to him after his death. Zayda b. Qudāma struck down the butcher Muṣʻab at the Monastery of the Catholicus with the words: "This is Revenge for Mukhtār!"

In the final analysis history has not to report on men's hearts, but to evaluate their deeds. Whatever Mukhtār himself may have been like, he nevertheless had an effect which cannot be overestimated.

Shī'ism in Kūfa at that time went through a moulting process. We have seen what it represented originally. It was the expression of a general political feeling, the opposition of Iraq against the Syrian hegemony. At first the Ashrāf went along with the others in that, and were in fact the ringleaders. But when in danger, they failed, and allowed themselves to be tamed by the government and to be used to suppress Shī'ite revolts. Thus they became separated from the Shī'a, who restricted themselves to being an opposition to the aristocracy and the tribal organization, more like a sect. As a result of the martyrdom of their heroes and holy men, they took on more of a fanatical character. Already the followers of Sulaymān b. Ṣurād had intended to revolt in Kūfa itself against the aristocracy of the tribes. Only Mukhtār brought this intention to fruition. In addition, he drew the Mawālī into the movement. This was an obvious step, because the movement, although until then supported by Arabs, had taken on a pronounced theocratic, non-national character and was directed against the born representatives of the Arab hegemony.[3]

Through its connexion with the oppressed classes, the Shī'a abandoned the basis of national Arabism. The link of the connexion was Islam. It was however not the old Islam but a new religion (Ṭab.II, p.647, 1.6, p.651, 1.2). It started from an obscure heresy with which Mukhtār co-operated - the so-called Sabā'iyya. They had anticipated a tendency which now began to predominate in ever wider circles, because the Shī'a was in general forced to a more uncompromising attitude against Catholic Islam and to a sharper emphasis of their difference. The Sabā'iyya are also called Kaysāniyya. Kaysān was the chief of the Mawālī;[4,5] if he was at the same time the head of the Sabā'iyya, then it would seem to follow that they were identical with the Mawālī (p.623, 1.14, p.651, 1.2). This lead was followed further and it was asserted that Shī'ism as a religion was of Persian origin, for the Mawālī in Kūfa were in the main Persians. Dozy says loc. cit., p.220s:

"The Shī'ites were basically a Persian sect, and it is here that the difference is seen most clearly between the Arab race, which loves liberty, and the Persian race accustomed to the servitude of the slave. For the Persians, the principle of the election of the Prophet's successor was something unheard of and incomprehensible. They knew only the principle of heredity. Thus they thought that as Muḥammad had left no son, his son-in-law ʿAlī should have succeeded him and that the sovereignty was hereditary in his family. As a result, all the Caliphs except ʿAlī in their eyes were usurpers to whom one did not owe obedience. The hatred which they felt for the government and for Arab domination confirmed them in this opinion. At the same time they cast covetous glances towards the riches of their masters. Moreover, accustomed to seeing in their Kings the descendants of minor deities, they brought this idolatrous respect to bear upon ʿAlī and his posterity. Absolute obedience to the Imam of the race of ʿAlī - such was the most important duty in their eyes. If this duty was fulfilled, one could unscrupulously interpret all the others allegorically, and transgress them. For them, the Imam was everything. He was God made man. Servile submission accompanied by immortality - such was the basis of their system." A. Müller expresses himself in similar terms, I, p.327; he adds that for a long time before Islam, the Persians under the influence of Indian ideas had inclined to the view that the Shahanshah was an incarnation of the divine spirit which, passing from father to son, inspired the ruling tribe.

There is no doubt that the Shīʿite ideas appealed to the Persians, but it is not therefore proven that they originated from them. Tradition speaks against this. According to it, outspoken Shīʿism existed much more in Arabic milieux, and only from there did it pass to the Mawālī and become part of them. Those people who danced around the holy chair were called the Sabāʾiyya (Ṭab.II, p.703, l.17, p.704, l.11). They were not Mawālī, but Arabs, particularly from Nahd, Khārif, Thawr, Shākir and Shibām.[6] These Sabāʾites, as a result of their strange religion, were on bad terms with the main group of their tribes, particularly the Shibām with the Hamdān, and they enjoyed a very close relationship with Mukhtār, for whom they went through fire and willingly betrayed their cousins. A Biṭāna[7] (clique or special group) of Arab Shīʿites is known about, which used to convene in the houses of two distinguished ladies. Names of individual members are given, amongst them being Ibn Nawf al-Hamdānī who vied with his lord and master in prophesying. He was a prophet of the holy chair, which also served as an oracle. An uncle of the poet Aʿshā Hamdān was impressed by this. Guardian (Ṣādin) of the chair was first of all Mūsā, a son of the well-known Abū Mūsā al-Ashʿarī, then Hawshab al-Bursumī. The *milieu* is totally Yemenī.[8] The chair is definitely supposed to have been produced on Mukhtār's command as a relic of ʿAlī,[9] but other more credible reports contradict this.[10] At all events, it was in the possession of the Yemenīs and its origin should certainly be sought amongst them. It represented no arbitrary invention but was a relic of heathendom like the black stone; it was originally God's chair and then the chair of ʿAlī because ʿAlī was deified.[11] Such empty chairs of God are frequently found, as is well-known, although they are not usually made of wood.

The origins of the Sabā'iyya go back to the time of ʿAlī and Ḥasan.[12] They derive from ʿAbdalla b. Sabā'. As one can already infer from his peculiar name, he was equally a Yemenī, in fact from the capital Ṣanʿā. In addition he is supposed to have been a Jew. Thus one is led to a Jewish origin of the sect. Certainly many things are called Jews and Jewish by the Muslims without any reason.[13] But in fact the dogma of Shīʿism, the founder of which is considered to be Ibn Sabā', seems to stem more from the Jews than from the Persians.[14] I shall occasionally point out indications of this in the following attempt to describe it,[15] without, however, attributing more importance to the whole question than it deserves.

ʿAlī's oldest supporters put him on the same level as his predecessors in the Caliphate. He belonged to one line along with Abū Bakr, ʿUmar, and also ʿUthmān as long as he ruled lawfully. He was opposed only to the Umayyad usurpers as the continuation of the lawful Caliphate. His right to rule resulted from the fact that he belonged to the aristocracy of the Companions, was put in the position of power by them, and received the oath of allegiance from Medina. This was not a result, or at least not directly, from the fact that he belonged to the family of Muḥammad.[16] Yet this family itself seems from the outset to have asserted some hereditary right to the ruling position, and after ʿAlī's death his sons were set up by the opposition to the Umayyads as legitimate pretenders. The point at issue then is only about the claim to the Caliphate. The claim to prophethood has to be distinguished from that. The assertion that prophethood did not have its end in Muḥammad but lived on in ʿAlī and his sons, was the last step.

The idea of the monarchic Prophet as the sovereign representative of the rule of God on earth passed from the Jews to Islam.[17] Now according to orthodox Islam, Muḥammad was the last Prophet, and after his death the impersonal Law, indeed a much inferior substitute, took over his position. That was a tangible break, and Shīʿite dogma steps in here. The principle from which it started was: prophethood - the personal and living representation of divine authority - belongs of necessity to the Theocracy, and survives in it (Ṭab.II, p.1061). Before Muḥammad, there had existed a long line of Prophets succeeding one to the other, as also the Jews accept an akribēs diadochē tōn prophētōn and just as previously, according to Deut. 18, Moses had never lacked a successor similar to himself. Nor does this line cease with Muḥammad. Every prophet has his successor by his side even in his lifetime (this zeugos is likewise Jewish), just as Moses had Joshua, so Muḥammad had ʿAlī, through whom the official position then is propagated. The name "Prophet" is in any case not applied to ʿAlī and his sons - they are called Wāṣī or Mahdī and generally Imām[18] - but in point of fact they are so, as knowers of the unseen and incarnations of the divine ruling authority. Also the line after Muḥammad was originally not represented as long, because in a short time the end of the world and the conclusion of earthly history were awaited. "The Imāms are four, ʿAlī and his three sons, Ḥasan, Ḥusayn and Muḥammad", says Sayyid (Agh. VII, p.9s.) or Kuthayyir (Agh. VIII, p.32). The last, Muḥammad b. al-Ḥanafīya remained alive until he had led the lawful cause to victory. Seemingly dead, he remained in fact concealed in the thick verdure of the ravine of Mount Radwā (near Medīna), where gazelles and lions lay down peacefully beside each other, and nourished themselves on honey and water.[19] He is beseeched in prayer finally to appear in order to console his true followers, after he had already left them waiting for sixty years (Agh.VII, p.10, VIII, p.32). Ibn al-Ḥanafīya had assumed the inheritance after the deaths of Ḥasan and Ḥusayn and was for some time generally recognized, for example also by Ibrāhīm b. Ashtar. He was convenient for Mukhtār as a puppet behind whom he could act. Even more conveniently, he allowed himself to be used like the old man of the mountains. He performed everything that was desired as a mere shadow, and then was unable to intervene in any way. His veneration was and remained the distinguishing characteristic of the extreme Shī'a (Agh. VII, p.4, p.5), the so-called Ghulāt[20] or Mufriṭūn. The 'Abbāsids legitimized themselves with the assertion that the son and heir of Ibn al-Ḥanafīya, Abū Hāshim, had transferred his right to them. As their tools they used the extreme Shī'ites in Kūfa and Khurāsān who called themselves Hāshimites after that same Abū Hāshim. The Hāshimites later joined the Rawandites, who also revered Ibn al-Ḥanafīya as the true Imām. (Mas'ūdī VI, p.38).

A type of philosophical substructure was given to the deification of the holy family by means of the doctrine of the rebirth, i.e. the palingenesis (raj'a) or the metempsychosis (Tanāsukh al-Arwāḥ). When death occurs, the spirits merely move from one body to another. It is a continuous process of resurrection in the natural course of the world, which differs sharply from the unique resurrection at the end of the world. But this doctrine only takes on its practical significanee essentially by laying emphasis on the spirit of God which inspired the Prophets. On the death of one prophet, it passes over to the other. Only one exists at the same time, but thousands of prophets follow after each other. However, they are all identical because of the divine spirit which is reborn in every one of them; in fact the one true prophet is constantly returning. In this sense also, the return of Muḥammad (in the 'Ālids) is claimed, and is based on the Qur'ānic verses Suras 28, V.85 and 82, v.8. One is reminded strongly of the very probably Jewish (although heretical Jewish) view which is expounded amongst the pseudo-Clementines.[21] The holy spirit combines with a human form in Adam and appears as the true prophet successively in various forms, and is destined to rule the eternal kingdom. (cf. Gieseler's KG (4th edition) I, 1, p.283.)

Later, as it appears, men understood the raj'a differently. They took the idea in an antithetical sense. They accepted a periodical eclipse (ghayba) of the true Imām and then in opposition to that, they called his re-appearance "the return". But the original sense of the raj'a is clearly proved by its synonymity with Metempsychosis.[22] Sayyid also believed in his own raj'a, and was brought up with that idea. (Agh. VII, p.8). In addition, he makes clear that Kuthayyir saw small prophets in all the children of Ḥasan and Ḥusayn, because he believed in the raj'a (Agh. VIII, p.34) and it is particularly evident that Muḥammad himself was thought of as returning again in the heirs to his blood and his prophet-hood.[23] Modern writers did not recognize or observe that. It is also likely that the old belief also disappeared, namely that the true Imām is always alive on earth, although not always in a state of strength and splendour.

The judgement on the Shī'ites pronounced by the Khārijite Abū Hazm during the year 130/747 in a sermon from the pulpit at Medīna is worthy of note and informative: (Agh. XX, p.107) "They assert that they hold fast to God's book, but they openly oppose it with their own trivial discoveries and do not arrive at a profound understanding of the Qur'ān, nor a penetrating knowledge of the law, nor an investigation of the pure truth. They disguise everything with their party interests. Their religion consists of devotion to a group whom they obey in everything that is asked of them, whether it is right or wrong, the false or the true way. They await a new era through the return of the dead, and believe in a resurrection before the Day of Judgement. They ascribe knowledge of the Unseen to a created being, a human being who does not even know what lies hidden in his own house, behind his garments, and within his body. They reproach tyrants for their crime, but will commit it themselves if they achieve power, nor can they avoid it, ignorant of religion as they are. They entrust themselves in matters of religion to an Arab family and claim that their client-relationship to these masters exempts them from good deeds and from the punishment of evil doers."[24] The Caliph Hishām expresses himself similarly in a letter to Yūsuf b. 'Umar (Ṭab.II, p.1682, l.5s.). The worship of God as practised by the Shī'ites was a worship of men, and this led to Caesaropapism,[25] to a veneration, as it were, of Emperor and Pope in one. They protested against the Imāmate of the present holders of power, but their own legitimate Imāmate of the prophetic blood was no better. It led to scorn of the law. The Imām was above the letter of the law and knew the Unseen; whoever supported him and obeyed him was absolved of his own responsibility. The Khawārij stressed this particularly - they who with greater determination than all others placed the universally applicable law above everything and measured the Imām according to that, before deciding whether he was the right man or not.

The transference of extreme Shīʻism to the Mawālī was an event of world-shaking significance.[26] Perhaps it was Mukhtār who found the Shīʻite Mawālī already in existence, but he was the one who raised them into the saddle and spurred them to action. Originally he certainly did not wish to stir them up against the Arabs. At first he pursued a policy of reconciliation, had the whole of the Shīʻa behind him and even attracted the Arab aristocracy which was hostile to the Shīʻa. He wished to remove the distinction between first and second class Muslims in a peaceful manner. If one blames him for that, then at least one has no right to reproach al-Ḥajjāj because of the fact that he on the contrary tried with all his might to preserve this difference. In truth, Mukhtār deserves praise because he recognized earlier than others that the existing state of affairs could not be maintained where not Islam but Arab origin ensured full rights of citizenship in the Theocracy. Had he achieved his initial aim, he would perhaps have been the saviour of the Arab kingdom. But the Arabs were not willing to see their monopoly curbed, without being forced to do so. Thus in the struggle against them, Mukhtār was compelled to make himself completely dependent on the Mawālī and the Sabā'iyya. The battle went against him and, in Iraq, the Mawālī were reduced to political death. However, the memory of the short illusory splendour of the year 66/67 (685/6) was still not extinguished amongst them and a remnant of their party still existed in obscurity. This remnant, after a lengthy period, formed alliances with Khurāsān where the Persian national strength had its own area, and it was there that the storm blew up which swept away the Arab hegemony. Thus Mukhtār was the predecessor of Abū Muslim. The spirits which he had summoned became too much for him. Despite his misfortune, his effect was gigantic, but it was not intended. The verdict that he betrayed his compatriots to the Persians, and therefore had justly failed, is distorted in more than one respect. He is basically a tragic figure, against whom we need not hold the same antipathy as his contemporaries.

---

1. According to Ṭabarī II, p.732, Mukhtār did not advocate this doctrine (see Sura 13, verse 39), but it was Ibn Nawf. That he, like the Khawārij, fought with Ibn Zubayr against the Syrians makes him neither a Khārijite nor a Zubayrite. For the doves, see above p.138. Dozy explains them as carrier-pigeons which were supposed to give Mukhtār a swift report on the results of the battle, thus rationalizing the false miracle.

2. That is to say, an imitator from a genuine prophet. (L)

3. This conclusion is valid only for the episode of al-Mukhtār. Shīʿism drew support from Arab as well as *mawālī* circles. Shīʿism was a movement directed against Umayyad rule and its supporters, sympathetic to the claims of the *mawālī*, but not opposed to the Arab élite as such. See Watt, Shīʿism; Cahen, Révolution ʿabbāside; M. Hodgson, "How did the Early Shīʿa become Sectarian", *Journal of the American Oriental Society*, LXXV (1955), pp.1-13. (L)

4. cf. van Gelder *loc. cit.* p.82. The later historians of dogma are undecided whether Kaysān was a Mawlā of ʿAlī or of Ibn al-Ḥanafīya, not knowing the true story.

5. The sect named after Kaysān, as a sect, comes into being after the episode of al-Mukhtār. The Sabā'iyya also belong to a later period. Wellhausen here follows the tendency of Arab historiography to project conditions of later times back to earlier ages. For the Kaysāniyya, see Watt, Shīʿism, p.163. (L)

6. This is confirmed by the undeniable testimony of contemporary verses of Aʿshā Hamdān. (Ṭab. II, p.704s.)

7. cf. also the Dabāba p.669, l.2.

8. Watt suggests that South Arabian traditions of monarchy inspired Arab sentiment in favour of a dynastic principle and a quasi-divine ruler. Watt, Shī'ism, pp.161-162. (L)

9. From the family of the Mukhzūmite Ja'da, a son of 'Alī's sister Umm Hānī (Ṭab.II, p.705, l.15 cf. p.672, l.6, p.703, l.2, l.8, p.726, l.7).

10. Thus he did not contrive the hocus-pocus himself, but the most one can say is that he was not displeased by it. He renounced Ibn Nawf. (Tab.II, p.706).

11. It is compared to the Ark of the Covenant. It was usually covered up; the covers were taken off only on ceremonial occasions.

12. cf. Zeitschrift of the DMG 1884, p.391, and Ibn al-Athīr III, p.330.

13. Mukhtār himself is called a Jew by one of his enemies (Agh. XIII, p.37, l.30. cf. again Farazdaq. ed. Boucher, p.210 ult. p.211, l.3, l.10, Agh. VIII, p.33, l.14, XIII, p.37, l.27, Ṭab.II, p.686, l.9.

14. See notes to pages 17 and 151.

15. It is based on what is said in Ṭab.I, p.2942 about the doctrine of Ibn Saba' and also on the verses of the old Shī'ite poets Kuthayyir and Sayyid, in the Kitāb al-Aghānī. What is found in later histories of dogma is essentially identical with this: they only made unwarranted distinctions between Sabā'ites, Kaysānites, Mukhtārites, etc., for they differ only in name.

16. Ahl al-Kisā Agh. vol.VII, p.7, l.7.

17. Prolegomena to the History of Israel (1899) p.226, p.256s., p.273s.

18. On the Mahdī, see Snouck in the Revue Coloniale Internationale I. He is almost the Arabic counterpart to the Jewish Messiah as ruler of the 1,000 year kingdom. Jesus on the other

hand appears at the last judgement, after the 1,000 year kingdom.

19. Reminiscent of Isaiah 11 and 7.

20. Wellhausen describes the doctrine concerning Muḥammad Ibn al-Ḥanafiyya. Ghulāt, however, is not properly the name of a particular sect but the term later applied to early Shī'ite speculative and religious tendencies. Hodgson, Shī'a Became Sectarian, pp.4-8; Watt, Shī'ism, pp.166-68. (L)

21. But the association (Syzgie) occurs according to the Clementines between the true and the false prophet, not between the prophet and his successor (Moses and Joshua). The latter form is perhaps older, but runs into difficulties with the rebirth. Elisha inherits on Elias's death the first-born's share of his spirit.

22. Raj'a means return in the same body from the dead and is not synonomous with tanāsukh - metempsychosis or reincarnation in another body. Wellhausen's point here is that ghayba, the return from hiding, is not a return from the dead and so differs from raj'a. Hodgson, Shī'a Became Sectarian, p.7. (L)

23. Ṭab.I, p.2942. The parallel between the raj'a of Muḥammad and that of Jesus is a misunderstanding. For Muḥammad does not return at the Last Judgement; this is asserted only of Jesus, and has a completely different sense. It takes place not in the present Aeon but in the Aeon (= world period) to come. cf. Ibn al-Athīr, VI, p.26, l.2s., Agh. III, p.24, l.9, p.188, l.9s., IV, p.42, l.28, XI, p.46, l.6.

24. Hence Sayyid was an incorrigible drunkard, but thought that a friend of 'Alī's would remove the stigma of wine-drinking.

25. Wellhausen takes Caesaropapism to mean the union of religious and secular powers. But the Shī'ite idea of the imām is not quite the same as Caesaropapism. The imām is head of state and foremost authority on religion. A Caesaropapist emperor, however, has administrative authority over the church but not supreme

authority over doctrine. (L)

26. The sects are always more determinedly religious and less nationalistic than the official religion which was linked with power and the ruling nation.

CHAPTER 6.

The Mawālī were kept within bounds by the government, the Arabs having become timid because of Mukhtār. All the Kūfans were inclined to Shīʻism only in so far as they opposed the Umayyad government. This, however, was not because of devoted and energetic interest for the house of ʻAlī (Ṭab.II, p.1258s.). The revolt of ʻAbd al-Raḥmān b. Muḥammad b. Ashʻath was undertaken for the autonomy of Iraq against the hegemony of the Syrians. The same applied to the revolts of Yazīd b. Muhallab.[1] The true Shīʻa remained quiescent for a long period.

The genuine children of the Prophet, the descendants of ʻAlī by Fāṭima, lived in Medīna, the city of the pensioned aristocracy of Islam. They were the most distinguished members of that decadent society and at the same time the most popular. As long as they remained well-behaved, they were spoilt by the Umayyads and were hated only by the Zubayrites and their allies, the Makhzūmites. Everyone was delighted to offer them his daughter to marry and they took advantage of the opportunities to propagate the holy blood. They were able to enjoy themselves in spite of all distress in the pious city of wine and singing-girls (Ṭab.II, p.1910, l.12). Certainly they did not allow their claims to lapse, but they did not pursue them with clear sighted preparation. They wished to have nothing to do with the radical, non-Arab enthusiasts and conspirators, but they left them to the ʻAbbāsids who knew how to use them. There were no genuine men amongst them; only the women had breeding, above all Sukayna bint Ḥusayn. Of the two lines, the Ḥasanids and Ḥusaynids, the younger one was considered the principal lineage, because Ḥasan had shamefully sold his birth-right, while Ḥusayn on the contrary had shed his blood for his. Ḥusayn's successor was ʻAlī b. Ḥusayn, who was spared at Kerbelāʼ, and thereafter kept out of harm's way. Of his sons Zayd and Muḥammad achieved prominence, then the son of the latter, Jaʻfar.[2,3]

Towards the end of the reign of the Caliph Hishām, the Ḥasanids and the Ḥusaynids quarrelled over certain bequests which ʻAlī or Muḥammad himself had made for the family. As head of the Ḥusaynids, Zayd b. ʻAlī appealed to the Caliph, and went to him in person at Ruṣāfa, with some of his relatives. At that time Yūsuf b. ʻUmar, the governor of Kūfa, had forced Yazīd b. Khālid al-Qaṣrī, the son of his predecessor, to make a statement about his wealth, and had extorted by torture the evidence that he had a considerable financial claim upon Zayd b. ʻAlī. Hishām now asked Zayd and his companions about this. They denied the facts, but still Hishām judged it necessary to confront them with the imprisoned Yazīd. So they came most unwillingly to Kūfa, and thus the spark fell into the barrel of powder. Yazīd repeated his extorted claim in front of them and they turned from Kūfa back to Medīna. Only Zayd did not go with them. After the repeated urgings of the governor, he also went away, but returned again from the next halting place in spite of the entreaty of a more prudent relative. The Shīʻites had joined up with him. They said to him that the time was fulfilled, that Umayyad rule over Kūfa depended only on the few Syrian soldiers who could not prevail against the 100,000 Kūfan armed men - indeed not even against the Madhḥij or the Hamdān or the Bakr or the Tamīm alone. He was deceived by that, but took good care to change constantly the site of his quarters. He married into two of the families with whom he found shelter. His stay there lasted all in all some ten months. During this time he made preparations to revolt and also recruited in Baṣra and Moṣul. In Kūfa 15,000 men enlisted in his army. The form of the oath of allegiance ran as follows: the Book of God and the Sunna of the Prophet should be taken as the rule of conduct, the unlawful tyrants should be opposed, the weak defended, the pensions given back to those deprived of them, the public revenue should be shared equally amongst those entitled to it; those who had suffered for their rights should obtain atonement, those sent out to the distant battle-fields should be called home, and the family of the Prophet should be supported against everyone who opposed them and did not recognize their right. But for many people Zayd was not sufficiently radical. He considered Abū Bakr and ʻUmar as lawful Caliphs, something very characteristic of him and the majority of his Kūfan followers, and at all events refused to declare them usurpers. Thus he could not condemn the Umayyads, or so the extreme Shīʿites thought and they renounced any obligation to him. They were therefore called the Rāfiḍa[4] (the apostates). Now they declared Zayd's brother, Muḥammad b. ʿAlī to be the true Imām and after him his son Jaʿfar although they themselves certainly wanted nothing to do with the Rāfiḍa.[5,6]

The governor, Yūsuf b. ʿUmar, did not live in Kūfa but in Ḥīra, where the majority of the Syrian troops also were. Finally he managed to get exact reports of Zayd's actions from two of his accomplices whom he arrested. He then learned that Zayd was bringing forward the date of the revolt as a result of this arrest and had fixed it for Wednesday 1st Ṣafar 122 (6th Jan. 740).[7] At his command, on the previous Tuesday, the men of Kūfa were called to the mosque, imprisoned there and guarded by several Syrians. They seem to have been quite content with this protection in the face of their own negligence. When Zayd wanted to set them free with the 218 men whom he had nonetheless collected during the extremely cold dark night before the Wednesday, they scarcely moved a finger and he soon had to withdraw from the Mosque because 2,000 Syrians from Ḥīra were advancing against him. He repelled them on the Wednesday, and by good fortune also held his ground against them on the Thursday, until in the evening they were reinforced by 300 Qīqānic[8] and Bukhāran bowmen.[9] These men inflicted painful losses upon the small troops of Kūfan warriors and at nightfall they withdrew into the city and scattered to their houses. Zayd himself was struck by an arrow and died as it was extracted, in a house in the Post street.[10] He was interred in the bed of a canal from which the water had been let out, and then allowed to flow in again. But the place was betrayed and the corpse dug up. The torso was crucified in Kūfa,[11] and remained hanging there until Hishām's death. The head was sent to Damascus and from there to Medīna (Abū Mikhnaf in Ṭab.II, pp.1676-78, pp.1698-1711).

Yaḥyā, the still very youthful son of Zayd, first hid in Nīnawā (on the Euphrates near Kerbelāʾ) with a bondsman of the Umayyad Bishr b.b. Bishr b. Marwān. From there he fled to Khurāsān. Until Ḥusayn's death he remained hidden in the house of a noble Arab in Balkh. After that he was betrayed and handed over. Walīd II in fact ordered him to be set free. However on the command of the governor Naṣr he was moved from place to place until he came to the Western border city of Bayhaq. Had he gone further from there, he would have come within reach of Yūsuf b. ʻUmar into whose hands he had no desire to fall. So he turned back to the east and fortunately was able to force his way through to Herāt along with his companions, although the officials of Naṣr were ordered not to allow him to pass. He went further from Herāt to Juzajān, but there he was overtaken by the pursuers whom Naṣr sent after him, and was killed in battle at Anbār. (Yāqūṭ I, p.370). On the command of the Caliph, the calf of Iraq was burnt and his ashes strewn on the water.[12] Soon after, Abū Muslim set out to take revenge for Yaḥyā and killed his murderer. (Abū Mikhnaf in Ṭab.II, pp.1770-74.)

Zayd perished in the same manner as his grandfather Ḥusayn. However, his death brought about a transformation amongst those, or at least among some of them, who had pledged faith with him and not kept to it. They became his devoted followers and called themselves the Zaydiyya after him. They differ from the Rāfiḍa in their support for the house of Ḥusayn.

The last Shīʻite revolt under the Umayyads stemmed from ʻAbdalla b. Muʻāwiya b. ʻAbdalla b. Jaʻfar, a great-grandson of ʻAlī's brother Jaʻfar who, therefore, was not himself a member of the holy family. In the year 126/743, he came with his brothers to Kūfa in order to supplicate Ibn ʻUmar, Yazīd III's governor. He remained there for some time and married a great-granddaughter of the Tamīmite Shabath b. Ribʻī. But as a result of the death of Yazīd III and the dynastic confusion in Syria, the authority of Ibn ʻUmar, like that of the provincial officials in general, was fundamentally shaken. In these circumstances, the Shīʻites in Kūfa made Ibn Muʻāwiya their leader and led him into the citadel.[13] The remaining Kūfans in addition gave him the oath of allegiance. Then they marched with him against the Syrians who were in Ḥīra with Ibn ʻUmar in Muḥarram 127 (October - November 744), but fled when the battle broke out. Only the Rabīʻa and the Zaydiyya fought bravely and still pursued the battle for some days in the streets of Kūfa, until safety and a freer retreat was granted to Ibn Mu'āwiya. (Ṭab.II, p.1879ss.)

Now Ibn Mu'āwiya went via Madā'in to Media (al-Jibāl); his support increased, many Mawālī and slaves from Kūfa and other places rushed to him. First he established himself in Isfahān but, in the year 128/745, went from there to Iṣṭakhr in Fārs and from there he ruled over a most imposing territory. The east was then without any ruler and whoever cared to seize power could do so. An extremely varied society collected round him, 'Abbāsids ('Abdalla b. 'Alī) and Umayyads amongst others, hoping to pick up some office or reward from him. Most noteworthy is that the Khawārij expelled from Moṣul by Marwān II, amongst whom were Shaybān b. 'Abd al-'Azīz and Sulaymān b. Hishām, fled to him (end of 129/746 or beginning of 130/747). Together with them he was defeated by Marwān's troops at Marw al-Shadhān and with that, his kingdom broke up, (end 130. Ṭab.II, p.1978, III, p.4). He fled via Kirmān and Sijistān to Herāt in the hope of being well received by Abū Muslim, but on the latter's command, was seized and smothered with blankets. His grave in Herāt was displayed and revered for a long time after. (Madā'inī in Ṭab.II, p.1976ss., Ibn al-Athīr V, p.284s.)

In these last days of Umayyad rule, the dividing lines became blurred; everyone - even though still of varying strengths amongst themselves - helped each other against the vacillating government. Shī'ite and Khārijite fought under the same banner. The Shī'ism of Ibn Mu'āwiya seems, however, to have been of a notorious nature from the very beginning. According to Agh. XI, p.75s., he was certainly generous, ingenuous and poetically gifted, but was also unscrupulous and a free thinker. He surrounded himself with heretics, one of whom was later executed because he denied the resurrection and claimed that men were like plants. There are old connexions between the Shī'ites and free-thinkers.

The 'Abbāsids reaped the benefit of these unsuccessful Shī'ite revolts. Their time came after a long period of waiting, after others had prepared the way for them and shed their own blood.

1. For a full account of these later Kūfan rebellions see Wellhausen, The Arab Kingdom and its Fall. (L)

2. A more detailed account of the period between the defeat of al-Mukhtār and the rising of Zayd b. ʿAlī may be found in Cahen, Révolution ʿabbāside, pp.307-315, Watt, Shīʿism, pp.166-68.(L)

3. Bayān b. Simʿān and al-Mughīra b. Saʿīd al-ʿIjlī were executed in 737. For the importance of the ʿIjlī in the Shīʿite movement see S. Moscati, "Per una storia dell'antica Šīʿa" RSO, XXX (1955), p.267. (L)

4. They themselves say that the name is attributed to them not only by Zayd but also by Mughīra b. Shuʿba (Ṭab.II, p.1700). cf. Ṭab.III, p.561, 1.3. The Kāmil, p.548, 1.10, Agh. III, p.24, 1.19, XII, p.23, 1.20, XVIII, p.59, 11.4s. Sabāʾīya is an older name, Rāfiḍa a later name for the same thing.

5. According to Agh. XV, p.121, XIX, p.58, certain crazy Shīʿites who already revolted one or two years earlier during the governorship of Khālid al-Qaṣrī had as their cry: labbayka Jaʿfar which implied a holy veneration of Jaʿfar who then was still less than thirty years old. But there is nothing of that in Ṭabari II, p.1620: there they are not called the Jaʿfarīya but the Wuṣafā (servants). They consisted of only eight non-Arabs, at their head the old Mughīra b. Saʿīd, an alleged magician. Khālid, who then was on the pulpit, was so affected by the report of their revolt that he immediately asked for a glass of water - this brought great scorn upon him. When the captives were brought to him, he had them burnt in the most cruel manner.

6. The distinctive element of Zayd's claim to the Caliphate was his repudiation of Shīʿite beliefs in a hidden imām and his declaration that the imāmate belonged to whoever of the family of Muḥammad actively fights to possess it. His compromise in accepting the legitimacy of Abū Bakr and ʿUmar was probably due to his effort to create a broad-based and effective movement. See Watt, Shīʿism, pp.169-70; Cahen, Révolution

'abbāside, pp.315-16; Moscati, Šī'a, p.260; and C. Van Arendonk, Les Débuts de l'imāmat Zaidite au Yémen. (L)

7. Wāqidī in Ṭab.II, p.1667 gives the date as the year 121. But the year 122 quoted by Abū Mikhnaf is corroborated by the day of the week; for only in the year 122 did 1st Ṣafar fall on a Wednesday.

8. Marquart, Eranshahr p.50.

9. By this period, Arab forces were heavily reinforced by local levies, some of whom were brought back to Iraq to form élite guards for the Arab governors. Qīqān was a place name in Ṭabaristān and in Sind, or Northern India. For the role of Persian forces in the Arab conquests see H.A.R. Gibb, The Arab Conquests of Central Asia, London, 1923. (L)

10. See Ṭab.II, p.1709, ll.5-6. (Ed.)

11. "We have nailed your Zayd to a palm-trunk and we have never seen a Mahdī (Messiah) who could be crucified on a tree-trunk". (The Kāmil, p.710).

12. Exodus 32.

13. Ibn Mu'āwiya won support because he was a member of the 'Ālid family. Not being a leading member, however, he fortified his claim to the leadership of the Shī'ite movement by asserting that the spirit of God had been transferred through the family of the prophet until it rested in him. EI, (new edition), I, pp.48-49; Watt, Shī'ism, p.170; Cahen, Révolution 'abbāside, pp.316-17. (L)

B I B L I O G R A P H Y

The following list consists of the texts used by Wellhausen from which he derived the material for this book. Where appropriate, the abbreviated form of the reference is indicated in brackets.

al-BALĀDHURĪ, Aḥmad b. Yaḥyā	Futūḥ al-Buldān, ed. by M.J. de Goeje, Leiden 1886.
	Anonyme Arabische Chronik (Band XI), ed. by W. Ahlwardt, Greifswald 1883. (Anon.)
BRÜNNOW, R.E.	Die Charidschiten unter den ersten Omayyaden. (Ein Beitrag zur Geschichte des ersten islamischen Jahrhunderts.) Leiden 1884.
al-BUKHĀRĪ	al-Jāmiʿ al-Ṣaḥīḥ, ed. by L. Krehl and T. Juynboll, Leiden 1862-1908. (Bukh.)
al-DĪNAWARĪ	al-Akhbār al-Ṭiwāl, ed. by V. Guirgass, Leiden 1888. (Dīnaw.)
DOZY, R.P.A.	Essai sur l'Histoire de l'Islamisme. (Trans. by V. Chauvin), Leiden and Paris 1879.
EUSEBIUS OF CAESAREA	Historia Ecclesiastica. See Opera, recogn. Guilielmus Dindorfius, Vols. I-IV, Leipzig 1867-90.
FREYTAG, G.	Hamasae Carmina, Vol.I, edited Bonn 1828. (Ḥamāsa).
GIESELER, J.C.L.	Kirchengeschichte. 6 Vols. Bonn 1829-57. (KG)

IBN al-ATHĪR, 'Izz al-Dīn	*al-Kāmil fī'l-Ta'rīkh*, ed. by C.J. Tornberg. Leiden 1866-71.
IBN HISHĀM, 'Abd al-Malik	*Kitāb Sīra Rasūl'-Allāh*, ed. by F. Wüstenfeld, Vols. I & II, Göttingen 1858-60. (Ibn Hishām)
IBN al-NADĪM	*Kitāb al-Fihrist*, ed. by G. Flügel. Leipzig 1871. (*Fihrist*)
al-IṢFAHĀNĪ, Abū'l-Faraj	*Kitāb al-Aghānī*. Būlāq edition, 1285 h. (*Agh.*)
MARQUART, J.	*Eranshahr*. (A.K.G.W., Göttingen, Vol.III, Berlin 1901).
al-MAS'ŪDĪ	*Murūj al-Dhahab wa Ma'ādin al-Jawhar*, ed. by de Meynard and de Courteille, Paris 1861-77.
al-MUBARRAD	*al-Kāmil*, ed. by W. Wright, Leipzig 1874. (*The Kāmil*).
MÜLLER, A.	*Der Islam im Morgen-und Abendland*. Berlin, 1885-87.
NICEPHORUS, ARCHIEPISCOPUS CONSTANTINOPOLITANUS	*Opuscula Historica*, ed. by C. de Boor, Leipzig 1880.
al-ṬABARĪ, Muḥammad b. Jarīr	*Annales*, ed. by M.J. de Goeje *et al*. Leiden 1879-1901. (Ṭab.)
THEOPHANES CONFESSOR	*Chronographia*, Vols. I-II, ed. by C. de Boor. Leipzig 1883-85 (Theoph.)
'URWA b. AL-WARD	*Diwan des 'Urwa*, ed. and trans. by T. Noeldeke in Abh. K.G. Wiss. zu Gött. XI, Leipzig 1863.
VAN GELDER, H.D.	*Mukhtar de valsche Propheet*. Leiden 1888.
VAN VLOTEN, G.	*Recherches sur la Domination Arabe, le Shī'isme et les Croyances Messianiques sous les Omayyades*. Amsterdam 1894.

al-WĀQIDĪ, Muḥammad b. ʻUmar — Kitāb al-Maghāzī, ed. by J. Wellhausen, Berlin 1882. (Wāq.)

WEIL, G. — Geschichte der Chalifen. Mannheim, 1846-51.

WELLHAUSEN, J. — Prolegomena zur Geschichte Israels. (1889)

YAḤYĀ b. ĀDAM — Kitāb al-Kharāj, ed. by T.W. Juynboll, Leiden 1896.

YAʻQŪBĪ — Historiae, ed. by M.Th. Houtsma. Leiden 1883.

YĀQŪT — Kitāb Muʻjam al-Buldān, ed. by F. Wüstenfeld, Leipzig 1866-73.

The following are the books and articles referred to in the notes added by Professor I.M. Lapidus and the editor:

al-ASHʻARĪ — Maqālāt al-Islāmiyyīn, ed. by H. Ritter, Vols. I & II, 1929-30.

al-BAGHDĀDĪ — see Brockelmann GAL, Supplementband I, pp.666-7.

CAHEN, C. — "Points de Vue sur la Révolution ʻAbbāside". Revue Historique. n.230 (1963), pp.295-338.

ENCYCLOPAEDIA OF ISLAM — 1st. edition Leiden 1913-42, 2nd. edition Leiden and London 1960-(in progress). (EI)

GIBB, H.A.R. — The Arab Conquests of Central Asia. London 1923.

HODGSON, M.G.S. — "How did the Early Shīʻa become Sectarian?" Journal of the American Oriental Society, LXXV, 1955, pp.1-13.

IBN ḤAZM — Kitāb al-Fiṣāl fī'l-Milal wa'l-Ahwā' wa'l-Niḥal. (Cairo 1317h.) For the English trans. and commentary of the sections on the Shīʻa, see I. Friedlander, JAOS,

XXVIII (1907) pp.1-80, and XXIX (1908) pp.1-183.

LANE, E.W. — An Arabic-English Lexicon (Reprint Beirut 1968).

LEWIS, B. — The Origins of Ismailism. (Cambridge 1940).

LE STRANGE, G. — The Lands of the Eastern Caliphate. (Cambridge 1930).

MASSIGNON, L. — "Explication du Plan de Kufa." Mémoires de l'Institut Français d'Archéologie Orientale, Cairo, LXVII, pp.337-60.

MOSCATI, S. — "Per una storia dell'antica šīʻa." Rivista degli Studi Orientali, XXX, 1955, pp.257-67.

al-NAWBAKHTĪ — Firaq al-Shīʻa, ed. by H. Ritter (1931).

SALEM, E.A. — Political Theory and Institutions of the Khawārij. (Baltimore 1956).

al-SHAHRASTĀNĪ — Kitāb al-Milal wa'l-Niḥal. See EI (old edition), Vol.IV, part I, pp.263-4.

VAN ARENDONK — Les Débuts de l'Imamat Zaidite au Yémen. (Re-issue Brill 1960).

VECCIA VAGLIERI, L. — "Il conflitto ʻAlī-Muʻāwiya e la secessione kharigita riesaminati alla luce di fonti ibāḍite." Annali Istituto Universitario Orientale di Napoli, IV, 1952, pp.1-94.

"Sulla denominazione Ḫawāriǧ" Rivista degli Studi Orientali, XXVI, 1951.

WATT, W.M. — "Khārijite thought in the Umayyad Period", Islam, XXXVI, 1961, pp.215-31.

"Shīʻism Under the Umayyads", Journal of the Royal Asiatic Society, 1960, pp.158-72.

INDEX